Aberdeenshire Library and Information Service
www.aberdeenshire.gov.uk/libraries
Renewals Hotline 01224 661511

8 - SEP 2008

1 3 OCT 2008

2 5 AUG 2010

-9 OCT 2010

- 8 NOV 2010

1 2 JAN 2011

0 2 MAR 2011

-5 MAR 2011

1 6 MAR 2011

-5 APR 2011

2.12.11

(MQ)

2/12/11

1 4 FEB 2012

1 2 SEP 2012

- 2 NOV 2012

1 2 FEB 2013

3 0 MAY 2013

2 1 NOV 2013

0 3 JAN 2014

1 8 NOV 2015

-9 MAY 2016

1 1 JUL 2016

1 3 APR 2017

WINTER, Dylan

A hack goes
west

A Hack Goes West

ON HORSEBACK ALONG THE OREGON TRAIL

DYLAN WINTER

Old Pond Publishing

ISBN 978-1-905523-68-9

Map by Eugene Fleury
Photographs © Dylan Winter

A catalogue record for this book is available from the British Library

Published by
Old Pond Publishing
Dencora Business Centre
36 Whitehouse Road
Ipswich
IP1 5LT
United Kingdom

www.oldpond.com

Printed and   ing's Lynn

Contents

A map of the Oregon Trail is on pages 18–19
A colour section appears between pages 128 and 129

Preface to the Second Edition

This was my second long-distance horse ride. The first was down through the borderlands between England and Wales. Being a stupid man, I thought that if I could manage two horses for 300 miles, then there should be no reason why I could not do it over a 2,000 mile journey.

For the British trip through the Welsh borders I had bought mares. Half-way through that journey I came out of my tent to find that one of them had produced a foal. So for the American trip I decided ahead of time to buy geldings as a way of guaranteeing that neither of them would be pregnant.

Which is how Rocky and Roland came into my life. I have worked with a lot of horses in my time and Rocky was easily the nicest. Easy going, sure footed and intelligent, but physically unsuited to such a massive undertaking as a 2,000 mile journey. He was, what the Americans call a perfect 'pleasure horse'. Great for kids, games and gentle hacking.

Roland, on the other hand, was perfect. Big, dumb, diligent and tough. But a rough bone shaker of a horse to ride.

Of course, I know now that I did it all wrong. I should have bought mules.

Would I do it again? Well for the first ten years after doing the journey I always said, 'never again'. But over the last few years, as I have got older and even more stupid, I have occasionally caught myself thinking that it would be 'nice' to try once more.

The trouble is that 'nice' is not a word to describe a 2,000 mile journey on horseback across the Great Plains and over the Rockies. It was hot and humid, at times it

was extremely tedious and it was tough on all three of us –
especially the horses.

My nether regions were bleeding.

I learned a lot about myself and about horses, but most of
all I fell in love with the middle of America and the people
who live there. It is an astonishing, alluring place full of sur-
prises and good, honest, kind-hearted people – which is
why I keep going back again and again. The space, the
sunsets, the night skies, the rolling prairies, the mountains
so clear, so sharp, so magnificent.

The next time you are planning an American holiday,
forget the tourist traps of the East and West Coasts. I suggest
you rent a car, buy a cheap tent from Walmart and ignore
the motels. Drive around and meet some real people. Go to
the craziest museums in the world, go to some real rodeos,
drive to a town with a name that sounds mad, visit a scrap-
yard, drive fifty miles up a logging road, pitch your tent and
drink in the real sights and sounds of America.

Never read an Introduction

Oregon originally belonged to the Indians. For a while the Spanish and the Russians thought they owned it. Then they backed out and left Britain and the United States to bicker and squabble over Oregon and its fur trade. For half a century our two countries shared the North West Territory in a unique trading arrangement where both were supposed to have joint ownership and equal rights.

It turned out to be a terribly one-sided partnership: while the British were represented by the mighty Hudson's Bay Trading Company, the American side was held up by a few intrepid, independent entrepreneurs. These small trading companies were thoroughly out-manoeuvred by the British at every turn. Whenever an American vessel turned up to trade with the local fur trappers it would be shadowed by a British ship. As soon as the Indians and mountain men paddled out with their canoes, barely buoyant under mountains of pelts, the British ship would move in and the Americans would find themselves being hopelessly out-bid by the British (those were the days!). Of course, if there were no American ships around, then the trappers and Indians had to take the much lower prices on offer by the British. Even though the United States and Britain were supposed to have a free hand in Oregon, the British dominated everything right up until the wagon trains started rolling into the territory during the 1840s. These pioneers had come 2,000 miles across half a continent and were determined to settle in this new land. The Hudson's Bay Company found it a tough job trying to persuade them to go elsewhere.

In the space of three years, the British contingent was

hopelessly outnumbered. The Hudson's Bay Company found itself surrounded by Americans and it feared for the safety of its warehouses. It decided to pack up and move its centre of operations to the relative safety of Canada. Which just goes to show that countries like Britain should not place too much faith in commerce as a method for back-door diplomacy.

Once there were enough American citizens in Oregon, the United States government told the British to relinquish their claim – or face the consequences. The Americans had already given us a bloody nose during the War of Independence and they had recently shown their willingness to fight for land by taking Texas from Mexico. Discretion is the better part of valour and all that – besides Oregon was an awfully long way from Britain.

So Oregon became part of the United States primarily because they managed to outnumber us. It was a classic annexation.

But where did all these Americans come from? What would motivate a man to sell everything he owned, buy a wagon, a team of oxen and set out with his family across miles of hazardous and unknown territory to a land he had never seen? It was partly, but only partly, down to government policy. The politicians did their best to persuade this huge mass of people to risk their own lives and those of their children in this great endeavour for something they called 'manifest destiny'. They wanted to extend American influence right to the Pacific – 'sea to shining sea' and all that. After a decade of political oratory and hyperbole, thousands of the mid-westerners who lived along the banks of the Mississippi did pack up and leave.

However, there were factors other than political hot air which persuaded people to move on west. The pioneers were hoping to leave behind a cataclysmic agricultural depression, rampant disease, searing mid-western summers, bitter continental winters, taxes . . . and politicians. The pioneers succeeded in escaping the lot – although it was not long before the last two caught up with them even in the virgin territory of the Pacific sea board.

But even the US government could not be so heartless as to send these pioneers off entirely into the unknown. Many had a government-sponsored guide – a book written by a man who had never been to Oregon.

The first group of pioneers hit the Oregon Trail in 1841: three wagons and a couple of dozen people. Two years later, a hundred wagons made the treck. That was in 1843, the same year that Edgar Allan Poe wrote *The Pit and the Pendulum* and *The Murders in the Rue Morgue*. It is odd to think that there was such a thriving, well established and sophisticated society in the east while there was a huge chunk of unexplored territory to the west. Within a decade, 50,000 people a year were taking the overland route west.

Of course there was an easier way of getting to Oregon: on a ship. But it was a long and expensive sea journey down around Cape Horn. If you had enough money to go by sea then you probably did not need to go.

The wagons used by the pioneers were known as 'prairie schooners' because their white canvas tops looked like the sails of ships as they lumbered across the ocean of grass in the great plains. The wagon boxes were three feet wide and ten feet long and their seams were sealed with tar to allow them to float during river crossings – of which there were many. They were usually pulled by six or eight oxen and could carry 2,500lbs of equipment and food. The equipment included rifles and ammunition, the metal bits of a plough, woodworking tools, kitchen equipment and a few treasured family possessions. The guidebooks also recommended that the emigrants should take 200lbs of flour, 150lbs of bacon, 10lbs of coffee, 20lbs of sugar, 10lbs of salt, beans, vinegar and cloth. Meat would be killed during the trip.

Better off families took two or even three wagons and a few family retainers along as well. One family called Ivins took four wagons. They had three packed with gear – the fourth was a spare and was done out as a bedroom with a large hair mattress with bolsters and pillows. A large box served as a table when meals were to be taken in the wagon. Of course Mrs Ivins would have been deprived of all this luxury had one of the other wagons been damaged. She does not mention any sleeping arrangements for her family and servants – many people slept on the ground under their wagons.

Another emigrant – Margaret Frink wrote in her diary:

> 'We had an India rubber mattress that could be filled with either air or water, making a very comfortable bed. We also had a feather bed and feather pillows. The wagon was lined with green cloth, to make it pleasant and soft for the eye, with three or four large pockets on each side to hold many conveniences – looking glasses, combs, brushes and so on.'

However, such luxurious accommodation was probably the exception rather than the rule. A wagon, all the essentials, a team and a few head of livestock for establishing a herd at the other end would cost a thousand dollars. This was at a time when a man's labour was worth a dollar a day. Most families could only afford one wagon. That left little or no room for living once all the necessities had been packed in. For many it was tougher even than that. Thousands of Mormons took to the trail with nothing more than a handcart of belongings.

One woman called Mrs Buck wrote in her diary how they came across a man who had returned from Oregon.

> 'Of course we were all anxious to hear about the country we were bound for, and our captain said, "Dr White, tell us about Oregon." He jumped up on the wagon tongue and all our eyes and ears were open to catch every word.
> ' "Friends, you are travelling to the garden of Eden, a land flowing with milk and honey. And just let me tell you, the clover grows wild all over Oregon, and when you wade

through it, it reaches your chin." We believed every word, and for days, I thought that not only our men, but our poor tired oxen, stepped lighter for having met Dr White.'

The pioneers had good reasons for taking the Oregon Trail. I could never fully work out why I travelled it. I have always been keen on horses and on watching Westerns on television, but I would be lying if I said that I had always wanted to ride the Oregon Trail.

1

Montezuma, God's own rush hour and beebling mopeds

'What about a gun?'

After a week in America the question no longer shocked me. Scared the willies out of me certainly, but I had been asked it too often to be surprised. The enquiry was not quite as simple as it seemed. I was not being asked if I was intending to take a gun on my trip along the Oregon Trail, for most people seemed to assume that not even an Englishman would be stupid enough to hit the Oregon Trail without any form of personal protection. They were just curious about what sort of firearm I might choose for a trip like this. Perhaps I had been mixing with the wrong sort of people during my first week in the USA. Horse dealers tend to judge society by their own imperfect standards of decency and fair play. They expect the world to reciprocate. There is a saying in Missouri that you would do well to count your fingers after shaking hands with a horse trader.

My first week had been spent driving around trying to find two horses which were tough enough to carry me and my gear along the two thousand miles of the Oregon Trail. During that time I had my wallet stolen, suffered a mild attack of Montezuma's revenge and was stopped for speeding – twice. On the positive side, I was let off speeding – twice, I bought two nice-looking horses and I met an awful lot of extremely good people, most of whom also seemed to think that I should be taking a gun with me.

I gave the gun question some serious consideration – for as much as fifteen seconds. I came to the conclusion that the world would be a much safer place, especially for me, if I decided to rely on my tongue rather than hot lead to get me out of a sticky situation.

So, right on schedule, a week after landing in the USA, I was standing on the banks of the Missouri river with two horses and a head full of doubts about what the three of us faced during the next five months of travelling. It was the last time I would be on schedule for at least a thousand miles.

My plans were clear enough. I had discovered that a group of people with half a dozen wagons pulled by mules had already set out along the Oregon Trail. The previous weekend they had started out from St Joseph twenty miles to the north of Independence Landing. By my reckoning that put them eight days ahead of me. I had assumed that one man with two horses, no matter how much of a green-horn he was, could travel faster and further in a week than a whole slow-moving wagon train. I thought that it might take me at worst a month to close the gap between them and me.

It seemed like a nice idea to travel with the wagon train for a while, the company would be good even though the pace would be on the slow side. Then, after a week or two of travelling in company I could set off by myself again. How wrong can a man be, but hope and optimism are such wonderful travelling companions. Without them few people would ever start out on an adventure such as this.

Of course, I did have some worries, and I was not short of advice. Everyone I had met had proffered it by the buck-etful – most of it focused on the dangers and discomforts rather than the pleasures and the beauty.

Everyone had their own personal horror. I had been

warned to keep my eyes open for marauding gangs of greasy-haired nutters on motorbikes, road-crazed truckers and local yobs in supercharged pick-up trucks. Few people told me what I should do when I encountered these hazards – other than to wave a gun in their general direction. Then there were warnings about snakes, insects and bears. The advice here was to run away, put up with it and climb a tree, in that order. Then there was the heat, dust and poisonous water. The received wisdom was to deal with these three by (a) sweating a lot, (b) putting up with it and (c) not drinking it. No one could tell me how to differentiate between water which was poisonous and water which was safe to drink.

All this was before I got around to the worries that I had managed to dream up all by myself.

An optimist would be able to extract a lot of comfort from the fact that 300,000 men, women and children had successfully travelled the Oregon Trail before me. A pessimist would point out that, actually, 330,000 people had set out along the trail – 30,000 of them had perished somewhere along the 2,000-mile journey. That is one grave every two hundred yards. Nice thought. Some people estimated that ten animals – mules, horses or oxen – died for every human being. It is hard to keep such thoughts under control.

I looked at my two American travelling companions and felt guilty about what I was asking them to do. One was a tall, big-boned horse with the most incredible colouring I have ever seen. His mane and tail were long, luxurious and the colour of polished copper. His body was a complete hotch-potch of blobs and splashes, not one of them bigger than a fifty-pence piece. Swirls of white and golden hair spread like galaxies across a background of mouse-grey. He had a proud aristocratic head, spoiled only by a permanent, slightly wary look in his eye.

I had been told that he had been one of a pair of

THE OREGON TRAIL

SEATTLE

Oregon
City

The Dalles

Pendleton

MONTANA

Durkee

Brogan

Boise

Snake

IDAHO

WYOMING

Blackfoot

Buhl

Pocatello

Jeffrey
City

Montpelier

Cokeville

South
Pass

OREGON

NEVADA

N

UTAH

0   100   200 miles

0   100   200   300 km

- - - A hack's progress

CANADA

Oregon
City

Chicago

New York

PACIFIC
OCEAN

Los Angeles

Kansas
City

Washington
D.C.

USA

New
Orleans

ATLANTIC
OCEAN

MEXICO

SOUTH DAKOTA

North

NEBRASKA

Platte

Fort
Laramie

Lake
McConaughy

IOWA

Chimney
Rock

North Platte

Lexington

South Platte

Paxton

Fort Kearny

OMAHA

DENVER

Rock Creek
Station

Independence
Landing

COLORADO

Tuttle Creek
Reservoir

Lawrence

KANSAS
CITY

KANSAS

MISSOURI

matching horses which pulled a coach. He had been called
Continental and his former harness partner was called
Cadillac – named after the American-made luxury cars.
Cadillac, I had been informed, had been sold separately, but
it is hard to believe that anyone would willingly break up a
pair of well-matched horses – any horse dealer would know
that they were more valuable as a pair than as two singles. I
suspected that Cadillac had come to a sticky end, possibly
on the front bumper of a truck. That may have accounted
for the worried look in Continental's eye. As a name
Continental is a bit of a mouthful. I called him Roland. I
don't know why. It just fitted.

The other horse was an athletic little creature – and ugly
with it. His body was pale tan with white splodges, white
socks clear up to his knees and a big white patch across his
face. He had a sparse but fantastically busy tail and a pathetic
apology of a mane. His right eye was blue and white with a
slightly mad look, his left was brown, soft and passive, as
though it had been borrowed from a dairy cow. Like Janus,
he had a different expression on each side of his face. He
had once worked as a bull-dogging and roping pony in
rodeos.

Both horses were ten years old, or so I was told. Aging a
horse up to nine or ten is quite easy. A quick look in their
mouth will tell all. After ten the science becomes an art. Just
to complicate matters, Rocky had a second row of teeth
down the right side of his lower jaw. If he had been a
human he would have worn a brace as a kid. His teeth made
him a messy eater. Rocky had so many things wrong with
him that he was guaranteed the number one position in my
affections, although I had only known the two of them for
three days.

Independence Landing, the place where it all starts, is
a narrow bank of sand near a bend on the greasy, grey
Missouri river. It is tucked neatly under a rumbling cement
factory, half a mile downstream of a sewage works and on

the eastern fringes of the sprawling and ever expanding mass of Kansas City. It is owned by the cement company. There are a few piles of rubble, some trees and a large tower where cement used to be blown down a pipe and into the holds of river barges. Now most of the cement is taken away along the railway which follows the river to St Louis. It is the sort of spot where lovers might come to park for a quiet canoodle, had the cement company not put a gate across to stop cars from getting down to it.

In heading west from here I would have to make my way through nearly forty miles of town streets before breaking out into the countryside. Independence Landing would have been a very different place during the 1840s, 1850s and 1860s when paddle-steamers laden with wagons, animals, people and provisions steamed and splashed their way upriver to ram their flat bows hard up on the sand beach. They disgorged their seething, noisy, smelly burdens on to the west bank of the river, which then marked the frontier of civilisation. As the wagons and equipment rolled off, the steamers would get lighter until eventually the bows would bob clear of the sand and set the steamers free. The paddle-wheels would churn up the Missouri mud as the steamers backed off to head downstream and the crews would clear the decks of cattle and horse manure in preparation for the next cargo of emigrants.

At 5.30 a.m. on that Sunday morning I envied those emigrants. Certainly, they were entering completely unknown territory. All that many of them had as a guide was a book which had been written with all the accuracy, honesty and attention to detail of the average holiday brochure. They would have to use their own resources to deal with two thousand miles of prairie, desert, mountains, disease, wolves, mountain lions, bears and angry Indians. They would have dealt with all these without the modern conveniences of telephones, American Express and a police force. Some people might have said that our journey would be a piece of cake compared to theirs but in the America of the 1990s the three of us faced a much bigger and more immediate threat to our health and safety.

Christians – thousands of them. Baptists, Pentecostalists, Seventh Day Adventists, Lutherans, Mormons, Catholics and more. In three and a half hours' time the Kansas City God botherers would hit the streets in their thousands and Rocky, Roland and I would be in the thick of it. I had been assured that their driving was worse than the American average. After all, these people know where they are going – in the ultimate long term. Their faith gives them a dangerously fatalistic approach to the hazards of the highway. They ask for, and give no, quarter. That was what I had been told anyway.

My second biggest fear was the police. I had been foolish to ask one of the officers who stopped me for speeding about the best way to take my horses through the city.

'In a trailer,' was his immediate reply. Once he realised that I wanted to ride them he agreed to outline a route for me. We spread my map out on the ample bonnet of his American-built squad car. He took a blue click-top biro from his breast pocket and as he pondered the permutations, his finger played with the top. The business end clicked in and out like the tongue of a suspicious snake. The clicking bothered me almost as much as the gun which was strapped to his ample waist. Once he had marked my route, he leaned thoughtfully back against his car and clicked his biro a few more times. He asked if I was ready for my trip. I said that I hoped I was.

'If you are going to take horses through the city you will be needing a parade permit, a one-million-dollar insurance bond against any damage you might do and a shovel to clear up any mess your critters might leave behind 'em,' he said.

If he was joking he must have been a brilliant poker player because he was making a damn good job of keeping a straight face. I assured him that everything would be taken care of.

I took local advice, admittedly mainly from horse traders. They told me to do two things. The first was to pretend that the conversation had never taken place. The second was to hope that this particular policeman was not roistered to be on duty on Sunday, 12 May. If he was, and he did stop me with the horses, then I would have to pretend that I thought he had been joking. I might just get away with it.

I expect that I would have been given entirely different advice if I had sought out priests or schoolteachers as my mentors. I had been contaminated and was starting to think like a horse dealer.

I dipped my hand in the Missouri – a ridiculously ritualistic thing to do. I climbed up on to Rocky and turned the horses up the hill away from the river and towards the railway line. It was well before 6 a.m. and I was perfectly comfortable in my T-shirt. I expected that by the time we were forced off the road by 'God's Own Rush Hour', all three of us would be hot and sweaty. The first bit of the trail took us up a dirt track, along a tarmac road for a way, across the railway line and into the cement works. It seemed a simple enough plan. Only two out of our party of three were entirely in favour. Rocky walked straight up to the railway line and across it without any worries at all. I felt a jerk on the lead rope and looked around to see that Roland had decided to stop. There was no chance that he was going to cross something as awe-inspiring and potentially dangerous as a railway line without being given a chance to assess it first. I thought I could tolerate a short delay at this stage of the trip, so Rocky and I waited.

Roland sniffed. Roland looked. Then Roland had a think, and decided that on balance, if it was all the same to the rest of us, he would rather not cross this particular railway line. I gave him a minute to change his mind. He did not need it because it was already made up. We must have looked pretty silly with Rocky and I on one side of the tracks, Roland on the other and the lead rope stretched between the two – as though hoping to stop the next train. I urged Rocky back over to Roland's side and tried driving him across with a wave of my hat and a toe in the backside. No.

So I walked the horses around in circles for a bit and tried again. And again. I got off, stood between the two horses and led them slowly towards the tracks. I whacked Roland across the rump with the loose end of the lead rope and he decided to go with the majority decision. As I climbed back into Rocky's saddle I wondered how many more railway lines lay between the cement works and Oregon.

Within half an hour we were travelling through the streets of Independence. It used to be a town in its own right but it is now a quiet leafy suburb of Kansas City and in the early hours of Sunday morning it is about as dead as a town can get. We saw more dogs than people. The peace and quiet suited us fine. Then at about 9.45 all hell broke loose – although perhaps that is not the best description of a traffic jam of impatient Christians. I have never seen traffic build up so fast. It was as though four football crowds had all been tipped out on to the streets at the same moment. Most cars were packed with families straight out of *Knott's Landing* – some of them were incredibly numerous.

Rocky was as traffic-proof as a horse can get. In England he would be described as being 'bomb proof'. Roland was slightly more cautious but he was still pretty good. Most people were extremely courteous to us and slowed down as they went past – the kids pressed their well-scrubbed noses to the windows to get a better look at the horses. We had one narrow squeak where a man in a yellow anorak on a moped puttered up behind us, sounded his horn and then tried to beeble along between us and the kerb. He took all three of us by surprise and we made a sudden veer out into the traffic. Luckily, the oncoming Christians were awake and managed to avoid us. It was a relief to pull off the road and into the car park of a burger bar. I tied the horses to a tree, offered them some water and went in for my own breakfast. I left the roads to the Christians while I worked out the next stage of my trip.

I had arranged our first night's stop at the Benjamin Stables, which used to be a sizeable dairy farm and horse ranch well outside Kansas City. The urban sprawl has swallowed up all the neighbouring farms and bit by bit the Benjamin Ranch has also been nibbled away by development. It is now a sixty-acre island of green in a sea of concrete. American shoppers browse supermarket aisles where the cows once did the same to grass – but Mr Benjamin has been well compensated. He has a fat bank balance and his son runs a string of polo ponies.

There are fifty or sixty horses on the ranch now. Some are boarders, some are rented out for riding lessons, but the ranch makes most of its money by holding country and western dances in the old stable barns. I had bought Rocky and Roland from here but not before driving all over Missouri and Iowa looking at scores of other horses. I chose these two because they were the right age, the right temperament and they knew about traffic. Nearly everyone I met over the next four months told me that I had paid too much for them – but they were still cheap by English standards. And they were proving well able to deal with the traffic, although Roland walked slowly. I hoped to be able to cure that over the coming weeks. Shows how little I knew about Roland.

As we came in through the gate at Benjamin Ranch, I saw three of the wranglers sitting on palomino horses. The cowboys had cleaned their shoes, the creamy-white manes and tails of the horses had been groomed, their golden flanks shone in the sun. They were waiting to greet the first of nine buses which were bringing 450 aged package tourists from Wisconsin. The wrinkled tourists were coming to the ranch to 'experience the west'. This was to include a barn dance, a hay ride and a 'demonstration rodeo'. In the bushes near the three men on horses there was a shovel. It would be used as soon as one of the horses dropped a few nuggets of manure. The package tourists were here for the image of the west. They were not interested in seeing steaming piles of reality.

A bus came past. One of the three wranglers stood up in his stirrups and waved his hat in the theatrical 'follow me over yonder' gesture which has been used in a thousand western films. He trotted off across the yard to show the driver where to disembark his passengers. I followed at a discreet distance, worried that my English saddles might break the spell. The bus hissed to a halt beside the barn door. The wrinklies wobbled down the steps on to freshly scattered wood shavings which smelt pleasantly of pine. They were greeted by two of the girls who worked at the ranch. In the time it took me to unsaddle and feed my horses I heard Susan and Cheri say, 'Hi there, welcome to Benjamin Ranch,' at least a hundred times. The ninety-ninth incantation sounded every bit as sincere as the first.

The first twenty miles of the trail had gone more smoothly than I had any right to expect. All I needed was ninety-nine more days like this and I would have it cracked.

I went to join the pastel-clad pensioners in the barn. They had catered for 500 and 450 had turned up so I had been invited to join them for lunch. A country and western band was doing its best to get the party going. Once the 'authentic western chow' had been consumed the pensioners were herded out again and were helped to climb aboard horse-drawn trailers for the three-hundred-yard 'hay ride' to the demonstration rodeo.

By seven in the evening the tourists had gone and the ranch had fallen silent save for the sound of the traffic rushing past on the North Blue Parkway and 87th Street. I sat on the bunk-house verandah with the wranglers and helped them attack an ice-cold twelve-pack of beer. They seemed nice men, most of them in their early to mid-twenties, but I did not envy them their jobs – shovelling horse manure, acting as mounted car park attendants and wet-nursing tourists all day. They struck me as a pretty dissolute bunch of plastic cowboys. It is strange how often you are forced to change your mind immediately after it has been made up.

The beer was just on the verge of running out when the phone rang. Ronny went to answer it. It was a 'call out'. The wranglers suddenly went into overdrive. Chuck, the foreman, started issuing orders. In the rush to get ready Ronny explained that the Benjamin has the contract for rounding up stray animals in the city. The police report said that some cattle had escaped from a promotion at a hamburger joint and were loose in a city park. One was said to be a bull.

Within minutes, two of the palominos which had been on car park duty and one buckskin horse called 'Geddam' had been loaded into a trailer. We all jumped into the back of the pick-up truck and headed off for the city park. In the next two hours my opinion of these men was completely transformed. On the way to the call out they told me that they had one or two of these jobs a month. They had been using Rocky for such work until I bought him. Last month a truck-load of pigs had turned over and the wranglers discovered, the hard way, that pigs are extremely hard to rope. They have almost no neck and can back right out of a lasso loop. They also have the unfortunate habit of dropping dead from exhaustion if they are made to run around too much. Being involved in a motorway crash and then being pursued and roped by yelling cowboys proved to be too much for many of them. Ronny expressed an extreme dislike for the smell of pig manure. Their bunk-house had needed a thorough fumigation.

Today's report said that the cattle had disappeared into a densely wooded piece of land in a suburb in the north of the city. Three of us were on foot and three on horses. It took half an hour to find the cattle, which turned out to be two cows. We cornered them in a gully created by a badly polluted city river. The wranglers managed to get ropes on to them but then came the hard bit of dragging them out of the wood and over to the trailer. A large part of the next couple of hours was spent up to our knees in dirty water. I learned that American cattle have less respect for people than their British counterparts. One of them made a pretty good stab at impaling me on her horn. I was only saved by Chuck, who had hold of the other end of a rope which was around the cow's neck. He saw what was going to happen, took a dally around his saddle-horn and spurred Geddam in the opposite direction. It did not actually stop the cow but the sudden jerk certainly spoiled her aim. If Chuck had reacted a moment later my trip along the trail could well have ended before I cleared the Kansas City limits.

It was a pretty rough affair – on men, horses and cattle. One of the cows lost an eye in the process of getting her out of the wood. It was a bloody and disgusting mess. Afterwards we all went back to the ranch for a shower and to remove all the ticks from ourselves and the horses. Then we went off to get drunk. A jolly good time was had by all. The cows were sent to the slaughterhouse the next day.

I had intended to leave Benjamin Ranch at first light on Monday morning but the wranglers persuaded me that I would be better waiting until after the real rush hour was over. Despite my throbbing head I was packed up and ready to go at nine. My hangover was peaking nicely as I rode away along the road which leads to the city dump. The steady stream of clattering and pungent bin lorries made Roland rather nervous. Rocky did not seem to care that much about them. At first they were going too fast for my own sense of security but someone must have put a report out on the CB system and most of them had slowed down by the time they reached us.

Then I had to take the horses under the Kansas equivalent of Spaghetti Junction and down a curving road which followed the Blue river. For the emigrants the river was their first natural barrier. Middle American rivers are fickle things. They spend most of the year sluggish and brown, trickling along the bottom of implausibly deep river-beds. Then once or twice a year, when the rain is heavy, they go bonkers and transform themselves into angry silt-laden foaming torrents. The emigrants had to make cuttings in the banks to lower the wagons down one side and haul them up the other. It was usually necessary to double and even triple up the teams of oxen to drag the heavy wagons out of the mire in the river-bed. For us it should have been a case of just clattering across a bridge but Roland spotted the water flowing underneath. He froze solid. I circled back and tried again. I got off, threatened him with the end of the lead rope and walked both horses across. I wondered how many bridges and railway tracks lay between Kansas City and Oregon.

At about 11 a.m. we crossed out of Missouri and into Kansas. One state down, five to go. Later that same afternoon we passed out of the town and into the real suburbs where each house had five or six acres of grass around it. The air resonated with the thrum of lawnmowers. One person stopped his machine and offered me a cold drink. He had three acres of grass to cut and it took him eight hours to get round it all – twice a week during the spring. The lawn-mower business in Kansas must be a big one.

I had fixed up my first few nights in advance by driving along the route beforehand in a hire car. No one turned me down. It was a comfort to know where we would be staying each night but that sense of security extended only to the first three nights. From there on we would be taking what we could find.

After two and a half days on the road I came to a place called the Lone Elm camp ground and was alarmed to discover that it had usually been the first night's camp for the wagon trains. My swing around the suburbs of the city had cost me a lot of time.

Rocky was walking out really nicely but Roland seemed to be locked into his slow ambling pace. He kept on falling behind so that every thirty seconds or so he had to put in four or five paces at the trot to catch up. This made the pack he was carrying shake around in an alarming way. If he did not learn to walk faster he would soon be developing sores on his back. The alternative was to make Rocky walk more slowly and if I did that, we might add another month of travelling to the trip.

As we left the city I began to notice the Kansas wildlife. Actually 'life' is not quite the right word. Most of it was flat, smelly and very dead — reduced to a pulpy mass in the unequal battle between organic matter and Detroit steel. Three days into the trip and I think I could age and sex a dead racoon on smell alone. Flattened snakes and unbelievably pungent skunk cadavers were also a part of the visual and olfactory scenery.

Worst of all was the occasional tortoise — or turtle — crunched at the side of the road like a discarded half-eaten Cornish pasty. Turtles demonstrate the same blind faith in their defensive mechanism as hedgehogs in Britain. They rely on the sort of protection which has seen both species safely through millennia of natural dangers and predation — only to meet a messy death as a side-effect of humans transporting themselves from A to B. But while car-smitten hedgehogs get squashed, tortoises fracture. Bits of shell can be seen scattered around the side of the road and sometimes it looks as though a timely and judicious drop of superglue could restore the tortoises to life — provided all the bits were there.

One sad sight haunted me for many miles afterwards and

I still feel like a wimp for not taking action. It was a female possum which had been hit by a car. Her corpse was largely intact and on her face was a strange look of surprised indignation. Possums carry their young around on their backs until they are quite old and this female had five young ones. Two had been killed when the mother was hit but the other three were still alive and were clinging hopefully to their dead mother's back. I should have stopped and finished them off but I was too squeamish to do the decent thing. I often think of the pain and distress of those three tiny creatures before they met their inevitable death from dehydration, a hungry crow or another car.

The weather was incredible. The temperatures were well up in the 80s or 90s and the humidity was about the same. The horses sweated hard and I was constantly wet. One night I tried ringing out a shirt but found that I could not dry it at all. It just stayed damp and started to smell even worse than it had before I tried washing it. One of my overnight stops was at a wonderful big house where the lady offered to do my washing for me. Judy explained that people do not bother with washing lines – a tumble-drier is the only thing which will dry clothes when the weather is like this. I left my new wallet in my trousers. She was too polite to say but I am sure that she did not think I would ever make it to the end of the trail.

2

A helping hand for Hitler, fastidious road builders and smiling mourners

We left the city behind and passed on into the Kansas farm-land. It was green and there were more trees than I had expected. The emigrants who came through here on the wagon trains said that the open prairie, with its rolling waves of flower-speckled grass, was like an ocean and that the flapping white canvasses of their covered wagons looked like the billowing sails of boats. They called them 'prairie schooners'. A big wagon train must have looked like an armada. Each wagon would have produced a small cloud of dust from the feet of the oxen and mules, and the wagons would fan out to avoid eating each other's dust, only coming together to cross a river or for safety at night.

Fifty years later a new wave of humanity came across here. They were Europeans, newly arrived in America from a crowded place where land had been parcelled up and labelled. Those who settled in this borderless country felt the need to tame and contain, to subdue and subdivide such an unimaginable expanse of land. Surveyors came to slice the prairie up into blocks a mile square.

Our gravel road headed resolutely west. It had a straight-ness and sense of purpose which would meet the approval of the most fastidious Roman road builder. I dropped into a travelling reverie about the lives of the people who used to live here a hundred years ago. The spell was broken by a field a mile or so ahead of us. It was brown rather than green, and not the uniform brown created by a plough but a splotchy brown. I could not make out what was wrong. Over the next fifteen minutes or so I watched the brown resolve itself into hundreds of discreet blobs with the bright green of the spring grass in between. A travelling speed of three miles an hour leaves plenty of time for speculation. It is amazing how the eye and the brain can scrabble for clues and come up with the wrong answers. For a while I was convinced that the blobs were bales of hay. Then they became chicken coops in an outdoor poultry unit, then tethered animals. Fifty miles an hour in a car leaves no time for such flights of imagination – something catches and confuses the eye and before there is time for the brain to get involved, it has come and gone. Just another half-remembered image.

The blobs became rusty tractors. Antique tractors, carefully lined up and grouped according to age and model. There was something terribly eccentric about them. Someone clearly liked the tractors enough to acquire and arrange them in precise neatness but there was not enough love left to preserve them. Time and the ferocious Kansas weather were slowly reducing this gallery of agricultural history to useless rust. I started counting and gave up when I got to the eighties. There was also a cluster of old trucks and some horse-drawn machinery, mainly mowers and rakes.

Half a dozen old horses and ponies shared the field with the machinery. But it was a big field and a wet spring and the grass grew clear up to the bellies of the horses. The field on the left of the road was grazed as tight as a golf-green – it was full of sheep, which was rather unusual in this part of America.

Up ahead a farmstead straddled the road. On the left was a higgledy-piggledy collection of buildings, sheds, old buses and lorries, all bursting with junk. A pair of circular steel grain silos, like an overblown cruet set, stood guard on one side. A few modern tractors and the occasional bit of farm machinery were scattered around the yard. The grass around the buildings and machinery was incongruously well manicured. On the right hand side of the road a white clapboard house stood under the shade of a couple of over-large trees. As I came closer I heard the sound of a peacock screaming its arrogance to the world. Nothing about the place added up.

Rocky and Roland needed a drink, so I decided to call in at the farm and ask for one. That is the beauty of travelling with horses, no one will ever refuse them a drink and while they sup and slurp you can tell your tale. People are then under an obligation to reciprocate. The horses are a licence to pry and probe into other people's business.

An ancient Chevrolet pick-up was parked under the trees beside the house. The truck was rust red, or it might have been red with rust. The door was open and an old man in washed-out blue overalls was watching us come up the road. He changed neither his expression nor his position as we approached. I got off Rocky and walked over. Dismounting to talk to a pedestrian is a matter of good manners – just as getting out of a car to talk shows respect. It is bad etiquette to ride your horse right into the front yard.

As I came close I opened my mouth to speak and was drowned out by a scream from a peacock. Roland jerked back in fear but Rocky held his ground.

I decided not to ask for water straight out and just said, 'Peacock'.

'Yup,' came the reply.

I let the silence lie for a while. He looked first at me, then at the horses and the pack, then back to me. Now was the time to do the introductions. 'This is Rocky, this is Roland and my name is Dylan Winter from England.'

'England', he repeated, as we shook hands.

Now it was my turn to reply. After a moment I said, 'Yup.' Just the way he had.

The man smiled with his watery-blue eyes as well as with

his mouth. He seemed to like my answer. The pick-up was old enough to be started with a pull on a cable rather than a twist of a key. The end of the cable was clamped between a pair of vice grips.

'Stanley is my name,' he said, giving no clue as to whether it was his Christian or his family name. It could have been both. It did not seem necessary to find out. I asked if I could water the horses and rest them up under the shade of the trees for a while. He offered me some oats for them and we sat on the tail-gate of his pick-up while we watched Rocky tuck straight into his bucket while Roland snorted cautiously at his. He finally decided that the contents were safe to eat.

Our laconically staccato conversation continued. I told Stanley what I was doing and why. He even asked me a few questions about getting through Kansas City with the horses. Then I started asking the questions. Initially I thought that I was embarking on one of the world's more memorable radio interviews. It was not so much that Stanley did not want to give anything away, he just seemed to enjoy the sport of having it dug out of him. He left long lingering pauses between answers. I started to do the same with my questions. A freeze-frame conversation.

'Tell me about the tractors then, Stanley. Why have you got them?'

'Like 'em,' he said. We left a moment or two for the birds to sing and the wind to rustle the trees.

'What are you going to do with them all?'

'Buy some more. Line 'em up.'

'Haven't you got enough yet?'

'Nope.'

Rocky finished his oats and stuck his head in the water bucket. His ears flicked back and forth every time he swallowed a mouthful of water. I counted the flicks. Fifteen. Just under a gallon.

'How many will be enough?'

More silence. A scratch of a stubbled chin.

'Hundred's a good number. Reckon. Don't you?'

'Then what?'

'Sell 'em maybe. Or maybe I will die before I get there. I reckon.' Stanley was spare with words. He tried to be dispassionate but the expression on his face and in his voice kept on letting him down.

I offered him some of the dried fruit and fig rolls I intended to eat for lunch. He declined. As I ate, I carried on digging away at him. He did not seem to mind. It turned out that he lived with his son, also called Stanley. The two of them rattled around in the white house like dried peas in a matchbox. They farmed two thousand acres, mostly arable land – just a few sheep and a few horses. The farmstead had been right 'purdy' at one time but a twister came and took all the farm buildings. The house was the only thing left standing. The storm had moved the grain bins clear across to the other side of the field. The Stanleys had moved them back again. The buildings were 'no more'n matchwood'.

The father and son also dealt in 'killer horses', buying up old family pets, promising a good home and then trucking them the six hundred miles to the USA's largest horse slaughterhouse at North Platte. The family pets and retired ranch horses would then be chopped up and frozen into convenience packs – the best meat going to Europe for human consumption, the rest going for pet food.

The horses in the tractor field were the beginning of a new batch. Stanley offered me six hundred dollars each for Rocky and Roland. He was only half joking.

Stanley then accused the British of eating horse flesh. During the war maybe, I said, but we are now like the Americans, too sophisticated to eat horse meat – we feed it to our dogs instead. I suggested that this must surely be a much higher level of civilisation. It was clearly the sort of black humour which appealed to Stanley. He very nearly laughed.

He went on to tell me how the Stanleys had been on bad terms with their neighbours for three generations. Part of the pleasure of owning the sheep, the peacocks and parking the tractors in the field was that they really upset the neighbours. He had once gone over to visit them and offered some meat as a peace offering. He let them believe that it was beef. He told them later that it was one of the horses which had been in the field beside their house. Stanley felt that he was winning the psychological feud.

'Be some smiling people at my funeral . . . reckon. Tickled to death to get rid of me.' Talk of death made Stanley almost loquacious.

He was limping badly as we walked over to inspect the neat lines of tractors. I was going to ask him about his leg but he got in first and asked me what part of England I was from.

'London,' I said.

'Dirtiest goddam place I ever saw. Is it still dirty?'

'Yes,' I said. 'When were you there?'

'1945.'

'Where did you get the gammy leg then, Stanley?'

He smiled at my use of the word 'gammy' and said, 'Got my ass shot off. Omaha beach.'

'D-Day,' I said.

'Yup.'

'Lot of Americans lost their lives,' I said. A statement, not a question.

'They were shooting paratroopers in the sky as they fell,' he said.

'Was it worth your while coming all the way from Kansas to save the necks of us British?'

'Nope.'

I looked across at his face. Perhaps the grimace on it was caused by the pain of walking, but then it might have been the memory of the carnage he had witnessed.

I asked him if he thought that the Americans should have just stood by and watched the British be beaten.

'Nope.'

'What then?'

'We should have helped that old Hitler a little bit. Reckon he bit off more 'n he could chew. If we'd helped him wouldn't have had the Russians to deal with. Would we?'

Stanley was right of course. But I pointed out that Hitler might then have turned his attention on America.

'Damn right he would. Then we would have dealt with him.' Talk of rusty tractors seemed rather hollow after such an exchange. I tried to get him to tell me about the state of the world in the wake of a German–American alliance. He refused to speculate more. On this subject at least, I had plumbed as far as Stanley wanted me to go. All I got was a mumbled, 'Damn Japs.'

After we had returned from the field, Stanley took off in the pick-up truck. I liked to give the horses an hour and a half break at lunchtime, so I lay down under a tree to sleep. By 2.30 we were back on the road.

Travelling at three miles an hour along the same dead-straight dirt road allows time for thought. My eyes strayed from the horizon to the verge and the discarded fast-food wrappers and beer cans. By day four or five I was becoming quite an expert. I would come across the occasional cluster of beer cans along a fifty- or sixty-yard stretch. I am not talking about half a dozen dumped in one go but hundreds of them, thrown out of a passing car by the same person making the same journey over several weeks, months or possibly years – a habitual drinker who would glug back an ice-cold beer on his way home from work. Being a person of habit, the beer would always be finished at about the same spot in the journey and the can would be chucked out of the window. Here was an outdoor laboratory for studying the long-term effects of sunlight on the printing on Busch or Bud cans. The peripatetic American beer drinker seldom strayed from his chosen brand – he was a good conservative American citizen.

Sometimes I would come across a shoal of cans where there had been a change of brand at some stage. The American beer drinker is being subjected to a media onslaught aimed at changing his life and persuading him to switch his allegiance to low calorie 'light' beers. These contain twenty per cent fewer calories than conventional beers and the hoardings and television advertisements show pictures of unbelievably slim women and wonderfully trim young men quaffing light beers with impunity. I imagined my habitual beer drinker feeling his beer belly pressing against his belt, toying with the idea of changing his drinking habits and deserting his regular beer. As pointless as the twenty-stone woman who munches cream cakes while fumbling in her handbag for the sweeteners to click, plip plop, into her coffee.

In most cases the flirtation with the new beer doubtless failed to produce the desired reduction in waistline and the arrival of the slim girls. His physique and life were unchanged – except he did not enjoy drinking beer quite as much. The evidence of brief dalliance and swift return to his old brand is written in the verge.

Reading the human history in the shoals of beer cans along the side of the road became such an obsession that I would stop the horses to take a better look. Sometimes I even retraced my steps to try to deduce more about these highway alcoholics.

3

Chasing the storm, working for Uncle Sam and caged seagulls

I saw from the map that the grid system of dirt roads was interrupted by a large man-made reservoir – Clinton Lake. Across one end was a two-mile-long earth dam. From the low side it was a rolling hump of grass, like a green tidal wave sweeping across the prairie. The map showed that there was a public camp and picnic site tucked away under the far end of the dam. It was just where the concrete spillway came through.

I did not fancy staying the night under the dam. I could almost feel the weight of water above me. Too many disaster films on the television. Besides, it was really too early to stop for the night – despite the seductive availability of water and proper toilets. But it was hot. A two-hour break in the heat of the day would suit both me and the horses.

The camp site was perfectly standard for the USA: acres of manicured grass, picnic tables, toilets, turnouts for cars, small shrubs and trees only just big enough to offer shade, and the inevitable barbecues. American camp sites always have barbecues. A British family on a picnic spreads a blanket on the ground and produces a meal of sandwiches and salad from plastic boxes, and drinks tea from a thermos flask. An American family expects to be able to light a fire. Father will then embark on the ritual of cooking the meat. The importance of the occasion will be reflected in the choice of meat – in descending order according to the occasion: steaks, hamburgers, or the hot dog sausages which Americans call 'weavers' or even worse 'weanies'. Lamb is eaten only by foreigners (and coyotes).

Even the most urban American family will indulge in the ritual of cooking outdoors. It can only be a throwback to the pioneer days. Father cooks over the open fire because his father did because his father did because his father was a pioneer and had no choice in the matter. A necessary fact of life has rolled on through the generations until it has become a vestigial ritual.

A dozen of the pitches at Clinton Lake were occupied, but there was something wrong. Americans are usually pretty tidy campers. These sites were a mess, with litter scattered around, discarded beer cans and even the odd bit of household furniture. A few sites had tents, some had nothing but a mess of sun-chairs, cardboard boxes, camping stoves and all sorts of other junk. It was as though the camp had been taken over by refugees. There were no vehicles in evidence – except at one site where a decrepit pick-up truck was parked beside a leatherette sofa and a kitchen cabinet. Nearby, a man was sleeping soundly on a camp bed in the shade of one of the diminutive trees.

I unloaded the horses and tethered them on long lead ropes so that they could graze. They needed a drink but there was no bucket. America's favourite hat manufacturer, Stetson, uses a picture of a man giving his horse a drink out of his hat. Mine was still too new to be treated so badly – besides it had cost me $17.99. I decided to risk waking my slumbering neighbour and see if he could lend me one. He was only dozing and noticed me approaching. He sat up and rubbed his hands over his unshaven chin like a man being got out of bed too early in the morning. He was wearing a baggy pair of shorts and a dark blue T-shirt. A flaccid white crescent of beer belly beamed at me through the gap between the two garments. By the time I got close enough to shake hands he was standing and scratching his bottom in a delightfully uninhibited way. He did not have a bucket but he did have a big aluminium cooking pot he offered us.

By the time I had watered the horses and was heading back with the pan, he had started to boil a pot of coffee. He offered me a cup, 'Or a beer, if you want.' I declined the beer but accepted the coffee.

He said his name was Rick Job, 'As in the Bible'. He was from Arkansas and the word 'Bible' came out like 'Barbie'. We sat on the sofa in dilapidated splendour and drank coffee. There is something deliciously corrupt about sitting outside on a piece of furniture which belongs inside a house. I answered Rick's questions and he answered mine.

Rick Job, like all the other people living at the campsite, was a 'storm chaser' – a member of a fraternity of itinerant roofers who would follow storms around the country. Two months ago the university town of Lawrence had been hit by a mother of a hailstorm. The golfball-size stones had done millions of dollars of damage to roofs and cars. Rick was just one of around 3,000 men who had poured into Lawrence to make some quick money.

I said that the local roofers must be making a fortune.

'They already have,' he said. 'Within two days of the storm they had sold their companies to the big boys, who bought them just for the name, the phone number and the listing in the Yellow Pages. Right now, them local men are lounging on a beach in Hawaii. The big boys offer the actual work to people like me. We do our job and get paid in cash every time we complete a roof.'

I asked Rick if he was good at his job. He told me that he was 'not bad, but quality counts for nothin' in this business'. The insurance companies merely wanted to get those houses waterproof again. It was the house contents which were valuable. It did not matter if the roof started leaking again in two years time. That would be for someone else to deal with.

There was no charge for staying at the camp site but there was a three-day limit. The local authorities recognise that, for the time being, the town needs the services of Rick and his friends. They turn a blind eye to their extended presence and the squalor they bring to the site. Lawrence needs new roofs. Rick's presence, his bits of furniture and his beer cans all over their nice picnic place is the price they have to pay. But Rick can only stay as long as he is needed. Once the roofs are fixed the police will be down 'persuading' him to get in his pick-up truck and find another storm.

'Once the roofing is done they will hustle our arses off of here so fast you would not believe,' he said without a trace of bitterness in his voice.

Rick said that Kansas is a three-day state: in three days he could earn enough money for a two-day drinking binge. Back in Arkansas or Oklahoma the wage rates were much lower. There he would have to work for four or even five days to earn enough money for a two-day binge. Texas is a two-day state, producing the perfect two to two ration of drinking to working. The roofs are flatter in Texas as well. When I suggested that perfection would be no day's work for each day's drinking Rick said that I was wrong. The Lord had meant man to work for his living. Anything else was a short cut to sclerosis of the liver. Rick was a man of principle. His standards may have been lower than most but he had them, and looked down on those who had none at all.

'What happens,' I asked, 'if you are halfway through a job in Oklahoma and there is a decent storm in Texas?'

'Then we collect our tools, come down off the Oklahoma roof, whether it is finished or not, get in the truck and head for a roof in Texas.'

Rick had been following the storms on and off for a decade. He had once been a marine, seen service in

Vietnam and before that he was a bull rider in rodeos. 'Used to break horses for six dollars apiece.' Rich showed me a picture of his two children and his ex-wife. I showed him a picture of my wife Jill and my son Jake. They were standing in front of our house. Rick looked carefully at the thatched roof and was incredulous when I told him that there were a dozen or more thatched houses within a mile of where I lived. He flatly refused to believe me when I told him the thatch would last for twenty-five years – fifty if it was made from reed.

The previous night, he told me, he had wired 150 dollars to Arkansas so that his daughter – called Temple – could go to basketball camp for a week. I asked if he missed his family, whether he was jealous of the men whose houses he was fixing up, envious of their lives, their wives, their children, their comforts.

'Sometimes their wives,' said Rick, 'but I can always buy sex if I want it. I miss the friendship of a woman but then I look at that man, his responsibilities, see him going to work at seven-thirty every day, coming home at seven, day in day out. Every third day he works for Uncle Sam and the tax man. Every third day I take off and go to the bar. I prefer my life to his. If I want to work, I do; if I don't feel like it, I stay in bed. Today I did not want to work, so I didn't.'

We sat and talked in the Kansas sun with the prairie breeze keeping the insects away. We were surrounded by all sorts of junk – cupboards, chairs, a bureau. It had come from garage sales. Bought cheap. He and his friends will use the stuff, then either burn it or leave it when they move on; someone will come and clear it up for them. Rich showed me a pistol he had bought at a garage sale for fifty dollars. He was going to send it to his twelve-year-old son who 'liked guns'. The pistol had come complete with a box of shells. It was a small gun, Rick called it a Husqavanie and said it was a collector's item. It still looked as though it could kill. Rick did not think it at all strange to buy a working pistol for a twelve-year-old boy as a symbol of fatherly love.

By the time I had repacked the horses Mr Job was back asleep under his tree. I spent the next mile or so wondering how I would feel if I was the stepfather of a twelve-year-old boy who was sent a present of a 'collector's item' pistol by his blood father.

The road from the camp ground snaked up and around the edge of the dam and then headed off north. My plan was to keep going for a few more hours and then try to find somewhere to stop for the night. That afternoon the pack saddle started to slip around on Roland's back. Perhaps I had not repacked properly after lunch or maybe Roland was starting to change shape as he was settling into his work. Every time it slipped I would have to get off and change something.

Pack saddles are terrible things with lives of their own. They might ride perfectly for weeks, never needing adjustment from the beginning to the end of each day. Then they suddenly throw a complete wobbly. With every step of the horse they work their way to the left; you get off to tweak this, adjust that, move the other, and the pack starts drifting to the right. You get off again to tweak the other, adjust this and move that, and it starts moving even faster to the left than it did before. You get off again, to tweak, fiddle and adjust. The more the pack slips, the angrier you get. The angrier you get the less subtle the changes you make. The slipping gets worse.

There are so many variables. A pack and a horse are a dynamic system in continual flux. The horse is changing shape as it loses fat and builds muscle through the trip. The girths are stretching with the humidity and wear. One day the wash-bag is stowed in a different place, or the toothpaste, the soap and the shampoo have lost so much weight that the balance is ruined. The damn pack starts to drift around again.

I suppose that there are people who can balance a pack saddle other than by trial and error. I suspect it is a skill which can be learned only by years of practice and mistakes. What is needed is a gentle, precise, approach. A tiny change followed by careful observation to see if it has made things better or worse. Then another change, then another, until the pack is riding well. It requires the nit-picking pedantic precision which gets people to the top of the class at accountancy school. I used to watch those television programmes where explorers go to the Himalayas followed by pack trains of hundreds of emaciated ponies and think, 'What a lot of pack horses.' Now I watch with awe as the packs stay securely attached to the ponies' backs – despite the fact that they are picking their way through river-beds and up mountain paths. I look carefully at the men in charge of the pack horses. Had these men with their sun-burned and wind-wrinkled skins been born elsewhere in the world they would have finished up as accountants and auditors, always picking away looking for that balance.

I was nowhere near their league. Here I was travelling through some of the flattest terrain in the world with a nice big broad-shouldered horse and a modest pack – and I was failing miserably to keep the pack straight and square on Roland's back.

I was off Rocky and readjusting Roland's pack for the fifth or sixth time that afternoon when I noticed a lady waving to me from the side of the road. I took the horses over towards the car and she asked me if I was planning to camp that evening. I said I was. She said that I had better not as there was a tornado warning out for Douglas County. She offered me the use of a barn to keep the horses out of the bad weather. It seemed a ridiculous suggestion that a tornado could emerge from this warm cloudless summer day but an offer of somewhere to stay was tempting, so I followed her instructions to her house. She was there to greet me when I arrived in her yard.

Sandy was a small dark-haired energetic woman. She peered at the world through large glasses and did everything at double speed. As I unpacked the horses I received a thorough grilling on my trip and the reasons for making it. She showed me two stalls where I could leave Roland and Rocky safely out of the danger she said was sure to come dropping out of the clear blue Kansas sky. She then took me up to her air-conditioned house and installed me in the guest bedroom with en suite shower and bath – not bad at all. I examined my sore bottom in the mirror. It was in a bit of a mess. I had blisters, and then blisters on my blisters. After only five days on the road I already had bloodstains on the saddle.

I stood and drank iced tea in her kitchen while Sandy spelled out the horrors of the Kansas climate. She told me how a tornado can come down and strip whole swathes of the countryside bare of buildings, crops, trees and livestock. For many early settlers the arrival of a twister was their biggest fear. The first thing that a homesteader would do when he came to the area was to dig a storm shelter where his wife and family would be safe from the power of the tornado.

Sandy persuaded me to stay two nights at her house to give the horses a rest day and so that she could take me to the museum in Topeka where I could learn about the history of the area. As she was telling me about the museum, a small portable radio on the kitchen counter started to bleep and a calm male voice talked about severe weather conditions in the area – thunder, lightning, heavy rain and the possibility of tornadoes touching down in Douglas County. I looked again at the clear sky outside and wondered if it were possible.

We did not get the tornado that night, although one did 'touch down' in the neighbouring county. Douglas County got a thunderstorm – with nobs on. At two in the morning I was woken by a huge crack of thunder. I stood at the window and watched the most extraordinary pyrotechnics display from the comfort and safety of Sandy's guest bedroom.

At home we might get five or six thunderstorms a year. There might be a dozen decent lightning flashes in each. Here, in the space of an hour, I must have seen a hundred or more. The sky was illuminated by fork and sheet lightning leaping from cloud to cloud, sky to ground. I had never seen, or heard, anything like it in my life. I remembered a few of the reasons why I did not like camping.

The next morning I was full of the power of the storm but Sandy and her family seemed to have slept right through it. They were as blasé about their weather as the English are about the age of their buildings.

I went down to see the horses. They came galloping across the field as soon as I called them. They soon learn the voice of food. Roland really was a magnificent sight. He carries himself splendidly when he feels like it and he has a beautiful head. His mane can sometimes take on an almost unnatural orange glow when the sun is low down in the horizon. Rocky looks a rough-bred animal by comparison but he is more agile and faster. He arrived first and did not put on the brakes until the very last minute. He tucked his back legs underneath his body, shoved his front feet out in front and executed a perfect sliding stop. Roland arrived a few seconds later, with more dignity but a good deal less *élan*.

The two horses tackled their food in different ways as well. Rocky's strange arrangement of teeth made him a sloppy eater but his technique did not help much. He would bury his nose deep into the grain, grab a huge mouthful and raise his head to admire the scenery while he munched – wasting almost as much as he consumed. Roland would take his time with his food. It would be sniffed at and then nibbled to test if it was acceptable. Once he had settled his head in the bucket it would not move out until every grain had been consumed and the bucket licked clean.

As the horses ate, I leaned on the field gate and looked across the Kansas countryside. It was green and well wooded. The air was damp and almost cool after the rain. I was beginning to feel good about the trip. Granted, I was not making particularly great progress but I was having a wonderful time. So far so good.

Disasters are spiteful things. They wait until you are feeling good about the world before they come wading in to spoil everything. I should have learned by now to be particularly vigilant when I am feeling good. I turned my back on the gate and looked up towards the house, which was large and modern. It was built back into the side of a hill and had landscaped gardens all around. An extremely nice place. I was thinking what a lucky person I was when I became aware of a commotion behind me. Rocky had finished his food and was moving in on Roland's. The two horses started kicking out at each other. It was supposed to be a pretty formalised affair. Rocky was just trying it on, and Roland put in a kick to prove that he was top dog. Under normal circumstances that would have been that and everything would have been forgotten. But Roland got in a lucky blow and caught Rocky right up under the last joint on his foot. Rocky hopped away with blood spurting from his wound.

An hour later the vet arrived with his two assistants. All three of them wore T-shirts, pointy boots and jeans. Don put a stitch in Rocky's severed artery, pumped him up with drugs, told me that he would need at least ten days before he was fit for the road again and left with a wallet full of money which had once been mine.

Sandy and I talked the situation over. I decided that I could not really wait another ten days. Sandy offered to keep Rocky at her place while I walked on with Roland. She said that once Rocky was better she would put him in a trailer and catch up with me. By then I should be more than 150 miles further west and more than ready to climb back into the saddle. I had hoped to have got further before hitting a problem like this, but the walking would do me good, and my bottom was awfully sore. Technically it was cheating but it was either that or take the delay and increase the risk of getting caught in the snow in the mountains at the end of the trip.

The next morning Roland and I walked off along the dirt road leaving a mournful Rocky standing in Sandy's barn. I had also left a few luxuries behind, like half my food, a few clothes, my sleeping mat and my radio, the spare tape-recorder and anything else I thought I could leave now that I was down to one horse. I began to realise how much gear I had been packing into the saddle bags on Rocky.

The walking was rather pleasant. It was nice to have the pressure off my raw bottom and in some ways it is possible to feel more companionable towards a horse if you are walking alongside it rather than riding on it. Several times I caught myself talking to Roland.

By mid-morning I was five miles from a town called Lecompton. Actually the signs told me that it was 'Historic Lecompton'. There seemed to be an unusually large number of roads in the countryside surrounding the town. They all had names and numbers, and some of them were called streets, which seemed rather grand for dirt tracks which ran through farmland. It became apparent that someone had great plans for Lecompton. Roland and I were walking through the outskirts of a town which never grew up. Historic Lecompton was a Peter Pan of a town.

As we walked through its centre, I saw that it had a 'Historic Museum'. My legs were getting tired and Roland probably needed a rest, so I went to find the museum, hoping it would be a cool place. It was a whitewashed stone building, almost a mini White House. I parked Roland under a tree and joined a party of pastel-coloured pensioners being given a tour around the place by a chap called Paul Bonmar.

Lecompton should have been the capital of Kansas. It had expected to be. The impressive grid system of roads had been laid out to accommodate the thousands of people who would come to live at the mighty metropolis. Land speculators piled into the place and bought everything that did not move. At one time the town had a population of four thousand. Now it is around a fifth of that.

Its name used to be Bald Eagle but the city fathers thought that was unfitting for a state capital, so they renamed it after one of the richer locals – I am confident that Judge Lecompton had the honour thrust upon him much against his will. They also kicked all the prostitutes out of town and sent them across the Kansas River to Rising Sun City. Those in need of the unique services on offer faced a long, mosquito-pestered wade across the half-mile-wide river in the summer or a hard paddle in a canoe when it was in flood during the winter. The wives of Lecompton kept a careful eye on their menfolk for the telltale signs of an overdeveloped paddle arm or wet turnups, sure signs of a wandering husband.

Lecompton was deprived of greatness when the Kansans decided to draw up a pro-slavery constitution. Some people say that this was the spark which ignited the American Civil War. The government in Washington DC was split over whether to accept or reject the pro-slavery Lecompton Constitution and they debated the document for over a year. It became the focus of the growing rift between the pro- and anti-slavery states. Then America inflicted a disgusting civil war on itself. The technology of death was state of the art for the 1860s but the military strategies were straight out of textbooks on medieval warfare. The slaughter was on an unprecedented scale.

Lecompton's copybook was for ever blighted by its close association with the five years of pointless bloodshed and the capital was moved twenty miles up river to Topeka. The only saving grace of the sad affair is that several thousand property developers and land speculators lost their shirts.

The town once had a university, named after a man called Lane. He was not a great scholar – he gave more cash than anyone else to establish the place. Eisenhower's parents met there. Now Lecompton has even lost its school. Its children are bussed across the river to Perry. The pastel pensioners seemed more interested in the bits about Eisenhower's parents than they were about the town's role in the outbreak of the civil war. But then *Dallas* always gets better ratings than documentaries.

Getting across the river should have been easier for me than it had been for the philandering husbands of Bald Eagle or Lecompton. There is now a fine broad bridge. However, Roland demonstrated his customary caution over bridges. This time there was no Rocky to lead the way and assure him that it was safe. If I had been riding Rocky then he would have followed, stepping cautiously and with his eyes bulging with fear. But Rocky was fifteen miles behind and Roland clearly trusted Rocky more than he trusted me. He balked at walking on to the half-mile bridge. I managed to get him a third of the way across when we came to an expansion joint. Roland could see the Kansas river through the gap and he refused to go any further.

I walked him back to the bank, then turned him around and tried again. Roland stopped further away from the expansion joint. I turned him around and came back again. Still no joy. A man in a pick-up truck asked me if I wanted any help. His wife drove in front to warn oncoming traffic while he led Roland and I bashed away at Roland's rump with my cowboy hat. Roland put up a good fight at the expansion joint and I thought that we were going to fail when a man in a big articulated lorry came up behind us. It had a fine set of air horns on the top. Initially he kept well back, enjoying the sport, but I beckoned him on. He came closer. Roland dug in. The trucker gunned his engine, Roland moved a bit. I pointed to the trucker's air horns and made a motion like pulling a toilet chain. A blast of sound came out, Roland jumped clear over the expansion joint. He had a truck in front of him, and an even bigger one behind. It was a bizarre little procession.

That afternoon we carried on north past Perry Lake. It is another man-made affair, twenty miles long and designed to prevent the Kansas river from drowning large areas of Kansas City. It has a huge yacht marina where hundreds of ocean-going yachts are moored – two thousand miles from the sea. Their owners can only take them up to the top of the lake and back, a day trip at most. The yachts looked pathetic, like seagulls in a cage.

The banks of the lake are scattered with good picnic spots where families come from Topeka to enjoy the outdoors. While the kids play, the men fish or drink, or drink and fish. I saw several black men fishing, a sight you seldom see in Britain.

It is quite a surprise to see how much drinking goes on in the countryside. I assume that this desire to head for the woods or mountains for drinking sessions stems from prohibition, when drinking at home or in public was a risky business. Americans at play are seldom more than ten feet from a cool box. Hunters have camouflaged coolers the size of beer crates, families have coffin-size coolers as though taking deep-frozen relatives on vacation. Preparation for a fishing trip takes on the appearance of a burial at sea as huge ice-chests are wrestled out of station wagons and into boats.

America was beginning to feel like an alien place again when a man in a pick-up stopped to ask me where I was headed. He seemed pleased with my answer and offered me a bottle of his home-made beer.

'You are a limey, you will like this,' he said as he pulled

the glistening bottle out of the pool of ice in the bottom of
his cooler. I pressed the ice-cold bottle to my forehead,
twisted the cap off and took a pull. I expected the slightly
sweet and extremely bland lager the Americans insist on
calling beer. What went down my throat was heavy and
dark and sharp. It was the closest thing to bitter I had tasted
for well over a month. It was marvellous. The beer and the
generosity made me miss home and feel welcome at the
same time.

4

Bullfrog concerto, Eddy Waring and a Federal offence

I found a good place to stay that night. It was on a small farm owned by a Korean War veteran who earned his living by 'throwing' or delivering newspapers. I am afraid I woke Bill up when I knocked on the door at five in the afternoon but he was perfectly civil about it. I turned Roland out in Bill's field and pitched my tent behind the barn.

I turned in early but I need not have bothered. It was the hottest and most humid night of the trip so far. I lay on top of the sleeping bag and sweated the hours away. It was truly horrible, like a sauna, only there was nowhere to go for relief. England is a mercifully cool country where you do not get hot and sweaty just by lying down.

I might still have slept had it not been for the bullfrogs which kept up their 'rrrrub, rrrrub, rrrub' noise for most of the night. They took turns at serenading each other, expressing their willingness for sex or for a fight or possibly both at the same time for all I know. One would start and keep singing for three or four minutes. The solo performance would be followed by a moment or two of respectful and glorious silence before another frog stepped forward to take the microphone. I suppose there were three or four of them around the tent, taking turns. Their voices ranged from deep basso profundo to a top of the range tenor. Sometimes the respectful silence between numbers would stretch to two or three minutes. I silently rejoiced that they had come to the end of their repertoire. Then another would start up. It was like the Chinese water torture. I tossed and turned and cursed the bullfrogs of America.

I did once leave the tent to see if I could chase them away. The frogs fell silent as soon as I started walking around. The field where I hoped Roland was still grazing was alight with the flickering illuminations of fireflies, their tail lights shining for a second or two as they flew across the top of the long grass. There were millions of them broadcasting their desire for a suitable partner. It looked beautiful. And it was such a quiet way of going about the business of procreation – much more camper-friendly than the damned frogs. I would have stayed out longer to watch the display but the mosquitoes were starting to feast on me. As soon as I returned to the tent the frogs started up again.

Daylight came so I got up and called Roland over for his feed. He was limping. His leg was swollen and he had a cut on the back of his hock. He must have got himself tangled in a lump of stray barbed-wire in Bill's field. I walked him up and down a bit to see if he would exercise it out. It did not seem to get any easier for him so I put the kettle on the stove and put my head in my hands to have a think and a mope. I decided that I had to throw myself on the mercy of the lady who was looking after Rocky.

Three hours later Sandy had picked us up and the vet and his grinning assistants had been to see Roland. He told me that Roland would need a week off as well. Sandy told me that I was stuck and that I might as well enjoy my holiday. There are some people to whom you feel so indebted that you despair of ever finding a way to repay their kindness.

I rang around the car hire companies, including Rent a Wreck, Rent a Lemon and Second Hand Rose. All three had gone out of business but Rent-Sum-Wheels was in rude good health. Once fitted up with a modest car I spent the week looking after the horses, trying to stay out of

Sandy's way and learning as much as I could about Americans. I spent a lot of time at the museum and the library with my head buried in books about cowboys, pioneers and native Americans. I also discovered that the nearby town of Lawrence has an active rugby club. There are more rugby players in the USA than there are in England.

Strange to say, American rugby players have a terrible reputation for both consuming and spilling an unbelievable amount of alcohol, for singing rude songs, for taking down their trousers in public and for being thrown out of bars. The rugby players of Lawrence have bought their own bar. It has few soft furnishings and should be easy to clean down after heavy drinking sessions.

I met Louis, bar owner and rugby player of ten years' standing – and falling over. He told me that he had tried American football and objected to the 'mind set' which goes with the game. It has almost no social side to it at all. The teams are psyched up to hate the opposition as they travel to the game. They spend a couple of hours hating the opposition on the field. Then everyone gets on their buses and spends the return trip hating the opposition. Louis told me that rugby is an international game of three halves. Two are played on the field and the third in the bar afterwards, when valiant attempts are made to out-drink and out-sing the opposition. He has played rugby in France, Argentina, Australia and Britain. The friendship, the songs and the level of alcohol consumption were the same wherever he went.

Louis showed me the club house, which contained a number of typical rugby club treasures. One was a nicely varnished toilet seat which hung over the bar. A member of the club was entitled to place the seat around his neck to tell a joke. If everyone laughed they each had to buy him a drink. If no one laughed he had to buy a drink for everyone else in the place. There was a naked female torso and a trophy awarded to the member who was a 'model of hospitality and enthusiasm, who demonstrated responsible conduct in matters pertaining to the consumption of alcohol and whose actions did the most to facilitate hetero-sexual co-mingling by example'. I asked Louis if he knew who Eddy Waring was. He thought that he was a Scottish quarter-back.

I also went to an American supermarket and goggled at the range of food available around the clock. There was a huge range of meats and cheeses – most of which I had never heard of. A solitary live lobster lay sadly in the bottom of a tank of bubbling water, his hands taped together. There were over sixty different types of mustard, countless differ-ent types of bread, a special knife for removing the last bit of mayonnaise from under the lip of a jar, thousands of fridge magnets and well over 120 different breakfast cereals, including 'limited edition Cheerios with special tree-shaped green marshmallows'. I met one bemused lady shopper who said that her son would only eat a blend of two different makes. Fifteen thousand new food items appear on Ameri-can supermarkets shelves each and every year.

During that week I also managed to lock the keys in the car outside the supermarket. It was in the middle of a hail-storm and I was in a rush to get into the shop. I bought a steel coat-hanger and spent a fruitless half-hour fishing for the door catch while the Kansas clouds emptied themselves over me. I gave up and walked soggily and disconsolately towards the shop where I hoped to phone the hire car company. A young man wearing a black leather jacket and with long lank blond hair watched me from the dry of the shop porch.

'Been watching you buddy. Wanna hand?' he said.

'Do you know much about it?' I said.

'Some,' he replied. 'Let's just wait for the storm to pass.'

We stood and silently watched the storm die away. He took the coat-hanger out of my hand. 'Ford Tempo,' he said and started twisting the coat-hanger into a precise shape. He measured the bend in the end against his index finger and winked at me. Actually it was more a leer than a wink.

'Slightly different for each type of car,' he said as we navigated our way around the puddles in the car park. He moistened the coat-hanger with a bit of spit, slipped it between the door and the frame, waggled it around for no more than fifteen seconds and opened the door with a flourish and another leer.

I asked whether he did this sort of thing professionally, or as a hobby.

'Let's just say I supplement my income some,' he said. Under other circumstances I am sure he might have relieved me of the contents of my car. That day he had my blessing and an offer of a ten-dollar reward. He turned it down.

I bought myself a cup of coffee from a take-away place. It had a warning on the lid that the contents might be hot and advised that the coffee should be sipped with care. Presumably someone had taken the company to court for serving coffee hot enough to scald their mouth. America is a country of litigation and avaricious lawyers. Everyone hates lawyers. There is an American joke about the way that you can tell the difference between a dead skunk and a dead lawyer at the side of the road. The skunk would have skid marks in front of it.

Day by day the horses got better until I reached the point where I was taking them out for an hour or two both morning and evening. The vet suggested that I should try hobbling them to keep them out of trouble when I turned them out on to a strange pasture. I bought two sets of hobbles, which tie the front legs of the horse together – they are handcuffs for horses. The experiment did not last long. Roland was completely unable to deal with them and kept falling over on to his knees. I was convinced that he would hurt himself.

Rocky sniffed his manacled front feet. He shuffled around for a bit, working out that he could still move his front legs but not very much. He experimented to see how fast he could walk. Not fast enough. He tried moving both front feet together. It worked. He started bunny-hopping around the field and within minutes he was travelling as fast with them as he could without. As a means of keeping him out of trouble they were a complete failure.

Eventually it was time to go. I said goodbye to my new friends at the rugby club, the museum and the library. I took the car back to Rent-Sum-Wheels, packed my gear on to the horses and headed on west. I was now seriously behind schedule. I would need both luck and skill to be able to catch the wagon train – so far both had been in short supply.

We spent the first night of the resumed journey back at Bill's. The bullfrog concerto was as long and loud as it had been eight nights before, so I lit a candle and spent an hour or two looking at my maps and planning my route across Kansas. I wandered off into thinking about the names Americans choose to give their towns. Many of them have been imported straight from England. Kansas has got a Dover (two thousand miles from the sea), a Manchester (current daily temperature 98°F and no rain), Oxford (no university dons, no boaters, no River Thames), Winchester (no public school, no downs) and Reading (which might be infinitely superior to the original). I wondered about the people who decided to name their local town after one in Britain. They too must have dreamed their dreams of home, cool home, as they lay on top of their beds and sweated away the hot, humid Kansas nights.

The people who decided to call their local Kansas towns Moscow or Cuba could hardly have guessed what a threat those places would come to pose to their adopted country. Beside them such names as Glade, Green, Plainsville and

Rock Creek have a pleasing simplicity, and even more so beside the names stolen from the classics – Troy, Virgil and Ulysses. There is also a town called Climax, one called Liberal and even a Paradise, along with a Fredonia, a Kismet, a Woodbine and a Pratt. I had a passing whim to visit Pratt – but it was about 250 miles away from Bill's farm.

The next day we passed through Rock Creek. It is an extremely common American name – there is one in almost every state in the Union. Rock Creek, Kansas, was hot the day Rocky and Roland and I passed through there. The humidity shimmered between the white houses. Doors and shutters were closed against the heat. It was like walking through a freshly whitewashed ghost town. Actually, applying a British measuring stick, it was not a town at all – no traffic lights, no police station, no library, no drinking establishment. Too few houses, too few people. But in America even the tiniest cluster of houses is over-graced with the name town. In some places every house has disappeared and the only thing which remains is the name on a map produced by a cartographer who can't be bothered to go and look.

We had been on the road for three or four hours and I decided that Rock Creek could be our last chance to get water for some miles yet. The shuttered houses showed no sign of life until the last but one where a small girl rocked sluggishly back and forth on a swing under a tree. I tied the horses to a mail-box in front of the house. The mail-box had been bolted to the old stub of a telegraph pole. It looked good and strong.

I walked up the four steps to the front door. They were covered in bright green Astro-turf which bristled against the soles of my boots. I rapped my knuckles against the fly-screen and was instantly rewarded by deep guttural grumblings and the sound of over-long dog claws scrabbling for traction on a linoleum floor. The quietly threatening growl continued for a while and then slowly subsided to a deep, ominous silence. I knocked again. The threatening growl resumed but the pitch had dropped an octave or two. Then I heard a human voice growling at the dog to get back and the door was opened by a dishevelled, sleepy-looking man with a five o'clock shadow and a shirt hanging outside his trousers. I drew breath to begin my explanation but the words died in my throat as a rough-looking brown mass squeezed past the sleepy man. As the dog came towards me, the low growl rose in pitch and volume to become the fully fledged snarling bark of an animal with evil in its heart. I was confident that the evil was focused entirely on me.

It is strange how a sudden flow of adrenalin makes the world slip into slow motion. I had time to take in the snarling fangs, the scarred nose, the sheer bulk of the creature. I wondered how far I was from a hospital, I wondered about rabies shots. I thought of my own placid golden retriever at home who welcomed every visitor with the same amiable wag of a tail – even if they were collecting money. I started to formulate my best method of defence. I decided on retreat in the face of overwhelming odds but my legs were well ahead of my brain and were already dragging me backwards down the Astro-turf steps. The cur swept on past me.

As I staggered backwards I felt a wave of relief that I was going to survive intact after all. The dog was heading for a much larger enemy. Two enemies in fact. After all Rocky and Roland were tied to his mail-box, the mail-box which marked the edge of his property and which he had lovingly marked with his own individually scented urine almost every day of his life. These massive four-legged strangers had invaded his patch.

Rocky and Roland started to run away. I can hardly blame them as mere seconds before, faced with the same adversary, I had tried to do exactly the same thing. Unfortunately the horses were firmly attached to this strong-looking mail-box. They remained tied to it – but the dog's diligence in marking his property had taken its toll on the structural integrity of the stout wooden post. With a loud crack, it snapped off at its rotten base, swung up in a graceful arc and clattered noisily to the ground just behind the horses. As far as they were concerned this was a second wave of attack and they took off back through the slumbering hamlet of Rock Creek, dragging the clattering and banging mail-box behind them. The dog gave up the chase. He was more than happy about the dramatic effect he had produced and now felt pretty good about the world. After a few yards and bashes from flying hooves the mail-box proper became separated from the rotten post and the lead ropes slipped free.

This meant that both the dog and the mail-box had given up the pursuit. However, for horses, running away is an art form developed over hundreds of thousands of years of Darwinian evolution. Some might say that horses are designed almost exclusively for running away. Their main survival tactic is to panic, and keep panicking until they run out of breath. I watched the horses disappear up the road. It is hard not to feel upset when you are forced to watch all your worldly possessions disappear over the brow of a hill at thirty miles an hour. And giving chase to a runaway horse is a futile exercise. The dog walked back towards me wagging his amiable tail, deeply content that he had done a good afternoon's work.

I looked over at the man. His mouth was open wider than I would have thought possible. I walked over to the now well-battered mailbox, gathering scattered letters as I went. It was nearly all junk mail. As I picked the box up from the ground, the door fell off. I tucked the stub of the post under one arm and walked back towards the house. I handed the man his letters, his battered mail-box and his post.

'I am most dreadfully sorry,' I said. 'I will return.'

I am still surprised at my apparent composure. Inside was

panic, disappointment and dismay – a complete mess of
private despair – while outside I was behaving calmly and
logically. I felt as though I was watching someone else
through my eyes.

For his part the man still said nothing at all – although he
did make a brave attempt at closing his mouth. He nearly
succeeded.

I turned and walked back through the town. Many of the
once empty doorsteps now had people standing on them.
The horses had made quite a row as they thundered past. I
picked up a few scattered items of equipment – among
them a £700 microphone which had acquired a right-angle
bend, a ruptured water-bottle and one of the saddle bags,
which had been torn in half and was lying in the ditch. The
tape-recorder was still inside but it bore the marks of being
assaulted by a high-speed, steel-tipped hoof.

One or two people asked me what had happened. I told
them that my horses had run away. Two hundred yards up
the road I saw Rocky and Roland standing beside a
barbed-wire fence under a tree where two other horses
were sheltering from the sweltering sun. Roland's pack
saddle was hanging off to one side. I inspected the panting
horses for damage – one modest cut on Roland's leg was all
that I could see. I tied them up in the shade and stripped the
packs.

A man showed me where I could find a tap and loaned
me an old bucket to give the horses a drink. I then sat down
on my little pile of possessions to eat dried fruit and contemplate the future while the horses stamped their feet and
flicked their tails at the flies which buzzed around all three
of us.

Things were not exactly going smoothly so far. A whole
week lost to injury and complete failure to achieve my
target of one hundred miles a week. This last incident could
not even be blamed on bad luck. I should never have tied
both horses to the same post and I should have checked that

the one I had chosen was safe. Yet again my problems could be put down to bad management.

An hour later I had repacked the horses and was heading back through Rock Creek. I contemplated finding another way out of town to avoid the mail-box house but thought better of it. I had decided that a cash compensation was the only solution and was already reaching for my wallet as I approached the house.

The man, who was still unshaven, stood in his front garden. He was clutching a hammer but was smiling broadly at us. He had already replaced the mail-box with a new one. He started to laugh as we shook hands. He refused my money, saying that he had been procrastinating over replacing the mail-box since buying its replacement over two years ago. He said that he did not expect to have to buy any drinks in the bar that night and that he would not have to pay any bills for the next month or so.

'When they ask where their cheques are, I will tell them that they never arrived. You can't make a story like this up. There I was sleeping on the couch, a knock on a door, a red-faced man wearing funny boots is standing there. His horses steal my mail-box. He apologises in an accent like Prince Charles and then walks calmly off after the horses. I love it.'

He also explained that my horses and I had committed a federal offence by interfering with the mail-box. Next time I applied for a visa to the USA I would have to come clean and confess all. I remounted Rocky and headed off towards a town called Delia. We had to cross a railway line. I had to get off to lead Roland across.

5

Neon tentacles, plucking potatoes and miserable locomotives

We British turn our churchyards into gloomy sinister places by filling them up with dead bodies. The decaying cadavers are safely out of sight but the dilapidated gravestones are left as reminders of what lurks just a few feet below the surface. It has always struck me as being slightly odd to take wedding pictures of smiling couples standing happily amongst the aged gothic granite of our graveyards.

Americans allow the dead to make a brief final visit to church before banishing them to a well-manicured cemetery a healthy mile or two outside the city limits. This leaves churchyards free for more important things such as picnics, ball games and parking cars – and my goodness American churches need a lot of space for parking cars.

Most of these out-of-town cemeteries are extremely well cared for. The grass is kept immaculate, there are fresh flowers on many of the graves, and the memorial stones have a crispness and clarity of line seldom found in English graveyards, where the stonework could be three hundred years old.

It was memorial day weekend, when Americans make a special effort to pay a visit to the graves of their dead relatives and, perhaps more importantly, to their small town roots. People drive hundreds of miles over the memorial day weekend just to spend a few minutes in quiet contemplation by the graveside of a relative. It is one of the busiest weekends of the year for the roads; petrol stations have to buy in extra supplies of gasoline to see them through. The airports are clogged with traffic. On that single weekend, America burns more energy in travelling than some third world countries consume in a whole year.

Suddenly the pick-up trucks, which normally rule the rural highways, are outnumbered by city cars – Oldsmobiles and newer Detroit-built Japanese cars. The people, in their city clothes, looking as out of place as their cars, stand heads bowed beside the graves. They are usually older people, men and women in their fifties and sixties, mourning their dead parents, their own long-gone youth and, above all, the passing of the small-town communities which gave them their moral framework.

They drive around and try to remember what stood where McDonalds now spreads its plastic and neon tentacles. They see with sadness what has happened to the movie theatre and shake their heads disapprovingly at the girlie bars which have opened up – in a downtown where their biggest thrill was to drink Coca-Cola at the soda fountain. Other people visit towns which are dead or dying, towns where the banks, the hotels, the drug stores, have all gone, leaving just the post office and the one high-price supermarket. These people see their town and their past dying a little more with each passing year.

In many cases the cemeteries have proved to be longer lived than the towns which spawned them. Many times on my travels I came across incongruous patches of memorial perfection which seemed to have been built nowhere in particular – on the edge of just another field of corn. These are the cemeteries of towns which died in the depression or later, leaving no sign of themselves save a few ripples of distorted crop growth in a field of waving corn.

It was a record year for Millers. I do not know whether they are moths or butterflies but they are small delicate creatures with pale butterscotch wings. They settle on the hot roads, where their wings are a perfect colour match for the pale dust of the surface. There they sit, several score to the square yard, silently flickering their wings in the wind. As they move, tiny black shadows appear and disappear underneath them, making the road shimmer darkly ahead of us with each gust of wind.

The heavy footfalls of the horses created a shock wave of panic through the butterflies, which would rise up into the air above us and stay aloft until we had passed. They would then settle back to earth a few yards behind us. For miles on end we had a rolling, living wave of moths over our heads. I felt guilt at the disturbance we were creating in the lives of these peaceful, beautiful creatures. Then I saw a truck whiz past – its bonnet and windscreen were covered with a pale mush of crushed Millers.

One farmer told me that they would find their way into his barn at night. In the morning when he rolled the big doors back the Millers would fly out into the sunlight like a huge mushroom cloud of pattering wings. They were so dense they cast a total shadow across the yard.

We passed through a town called LeClede. No, it was an ex-town. LeClede is now just one farmhouse and one redundant school where the grass grows up to the windowsills. Two small sentry boxes stood guard in the bushes around the back of the school – separate but identical hole-in-the-ground toilets for boys and girls. I spent that night with a Catholic farming family called the Whites. Mr and Mrs White, now in their sixties, live in a brick house built by an Englishman. It would not look out of place in Hove or Hastings – except for the wide verandah around the lower floor. The Whites' three sons work on their immaculate farm. All three are married with families and that night the adults all came to supper to see the Englishman. The food was plentiful and good.

One of the boys had married a girl from Kansas City.

When she had first arrived on the farm Mrs White senior had told her to help herself to vegetables from the garden, especially the potatoes which were now ready to be harvested. Two days later Mrs White reminded her newest daughter-in-law to take potatoes from the garden. The daughter-in-law kept quiet: she had been to the garden and could not find any. Two days later she was again reminded to take some potatoes. This time she consulted one of the other wives, who took her to the vegetable garden and showed her how to dig up the spuds. 'You mean they grow underground,' she said in amazement. The Whites had all heard the story before but they laughed again.

There had once been many small farms in the fertile valley around LeClede. Now there were only three big ones. The Whites knew that their acreage could hardly support four families. If they were to survive, they would have to expand and that could only happen if one of the two neighbouring farms went out of business. It was a sad situation since the families on the three farms were good neighbours and the best of friends, but they were still fiercely competitive with each other.

Later that day Rocky, Roland and I crossed the Red Vermillion river. It was an easy crossing for us – although Roland jibbed at the wooden bridge. It would have been harder for the emigrants as they unhitched their teams so that the wagons could be lowered down on to the river-bed. It might have required three or four hours' work to get twenty wagons across this narrow river. The women folk would make fires and get cooking while the men worked together to get the wagons across, one at a time. And wherever the wagon trains were concentrated disease was sure to appear. In 1849 several trains were struck by cholera. There are over fifty known graves within a mile of the Red Vermillion crossing and hundreds more lie undiscovered here and further down the trail.

It is easy to believe that disease such as cholera could

thrive in this high humidity. Where the wagon trains came together for easy river-crossings the bushes and scrub all around would have been used as latrines. Wagon train after wagon train would have stopped here for the night. The good clean American families would unknowingly defecate death for the innocents who followed them. A thunderstorm like the one three nights before would wash the excrement with its deadly burden of microbes into the rivers for the next group to drink. Even those seeking to keep clean by washing their hands and their pots and pans in the river could be picking up contamination.

A man called David De Wolfe was passing that way. His diary entry for 31 May 1849 records:

> Got an early start, was joined by another company from Illinois consisting of horse teams. They had 13 men. We crossed the little Vermillion which has steep banks and a strong stream. On the bank of this stream there were six graves, all died with the colery (cholera) and out of a company of seven from Tennessee. We travelled this day on a fine level prairie all covered with beautiful flowers.

The prairie has changed a lot in the 142 years since David De Wolfe came this way. It is still good and level but the flowers have been replaced with a patchwork of crops and there are more trees now. Before farmers came here, the regular prairie fires put pay to any growth above the few patches of scrub along the edges of the rivers.

Rocky and Roland were losing that rolling butterfat of an out-of-condition animal. They were getting lean and hard with the work but Roland had one shoe which was rattling and Rocky had some unpleasant-looking cracks starting to appear in his back feet.

The Whites had telephoned twenty miles ahead to a man called Oscar Krause who does long-distance horse riding. He offered me a field for the horses, a bed in his cellar and a promise of a farrier to re-set Roland's loose shoe.

Oscar is a small man with a big Father Christmas belly which he zips into a pair of bright-blue overalls. He works at the local power plant, which had been dominating my horizon for the past two days of travelling. Its silvery slick smoke-stack pokes up into the sky like a rocket waiting for countdown. The power station burns coal which has been scraped from giant scars gouged into Wyoming a thousand miles to the west. The lumpy black energy is loaded into mile-long trains of over a hundred trucks apiece which rumble across the prairie at a stately twenty miles an hour. Four diesel engines thrum in harmony at the front and rend the air with long-drawn-out hooting wails of misery. American trains have to blow their sirens at every un-manned road crossing – and there are lots of those in the prairies.

Oscar's body spends its days at the controls of one of the 300-horsepower Caterpillar tractors which rumble around the manmade coal mountains of the Jeffery power plant in Pottawatomie County. Oscar has to make sure that the hungry maw of the power plant boilers never runs short of sustenance. While Oscar's arms and legs operate his Caterpillar as though it were an extension of his own body, his mind is free to saddle up his horses and head off west. He keeps it busy designing new and better pack saddles and thinking about routes to the Rockies.

Oscar and I sat on upended buckets waiting for the farrier to arrive. He told me about a man called Jim Brookover who had turned up on Oscar's doorstep three years earlier. Like me, he was travelling with two horses but he was fol-lowing the 1,000-mile-long pack-horse trail which leads from the city of St Louis clear through to Jackson Hole in the Wyoming Rockies. Jim was planning on bringing a full pack train through the following summer and was survey-ing the route. One of his horses had gone sick so Oscar had loaned him a replacement. It takes a lot of trust to hand a horse over to a perfect stranger and let him head off west.

Oscar's philosophy was simple. 'The only way to find out whether to trust someone is to trust them,' he said.

'And if they betray that trust,' I said.

'Then you know you were wrong.'

Oscar eventually got his horse back. Jim Brookover came through the following year with ten men and forty horses. Most of the horses were untrained mustangs gathered fresh off the foothills of the Rockies. The men were not that much easier to manage. Brookover's plan was to take his band through to the annual mountain-man rendezvous at Jackson Hole, Wyoming. He had loaded the horses with combs, trinkets and souvenirs which he hoped to sell at vastly inflated prices to the people who spend their holidays dressed as mountain men. He then intended to load his pack-horses with furs and make the return trip to St Louis. He was hoping to get high prices for the pelts because of the way they had travelled.

Jim Brookover had not reckoned with the American eye for a bargain. Even the fantasists who escape to the simple life by dressing in leather and living in tepees for a week at a time know the price of a comb in the local Walmart. He found that the modern-day mountain men were as canny as their genuine counterparts and refused to buy his wares until the prices came down. Brookover was financing the whole trip himself and was even paying his men four hundred dollars a month to do the trip. He ran out of money and had to sell everything, most of the horses as well, when he got to Jackson Hole.

Oscar had spent two weeks travelling with Brookover's little circus. He told me that it had been hard on both men and horses. Modern Americans are not used to living rough for long periods and the mustangs were causing a lot of problems.

Oscar also told me about two men who had passed through this way back in April. They were about six weeks in front of me and were travelling with two horses and two pack mules. They were hoping to get to Oregon.

He said that I should really have bought three horses for the trip. That way I could rotate them to give one a walking rest each day. He looked across at Rocky and Roland.

'It will be hard on them,' he said. We sat and looked out at the two horses standing quietly in Oscar's field. They were head to tail, flicking flies off each other's faces.

'It will be hard on you too.' He said it quietly, almost a whisper.

The farrier came later that evening and re-set the shoes on both horses. It was unfortunate that they needed doing so early in the trip. It was not that the shoes were worn out, just working loose. I did not know it then but I should have been taking more care of their feet by applying grease or hoof oil every day. Their hooves were drying out, allowing the hard material to shrink back from the nails. I was heading for trouble.

6

Defying physics, groves of marijuana and an elusive dream

We got a good start from Oscar's the next morning. Mrs Krause had sent me to bed with a full belly and made sure that it was filled again before I left her house.

It was nice to know that the horses' shoes were on good and tight when I set out west again. Rocky was still favouring his bad foot for the first half mile or so each day but he soon walked the stiffness out of it. I walked the first couple of miles before climbing up on to his back to settle down for the day's travelling. I was still having no luck with my campaign to make Roland walk faster, while Rocky was getting fitter and was keen to push on at an even faster speed. I had to keep holding him back. Perhaps both Rocky and I would have to resign ourselves to letting Roland set the pace. We would have to learn to enjoy the scenery more and relax.

The Kansas scenery was starting to get more wooded. The prairie was riddled with small streams and rivers as we approached the Big Blue river system. They must have made life very frustrating for the emigrant wagon trains. It was hard to believe but the humidity seemed to be climbing even higher. The radio had been issuing heat warnings and even the Kansans I met along the way were complaining about the unusual humidity and temperatures. It was around 20° hotter than it should have been at this time of year.

As we travelled along I began to notice an unusual deep-green weed, its spiky leaves with serrated edges waving ponderously in the gentle breeze. The swaying heads of *Cannabis sativa* stood two feet clear of the rapidly yellowing cereal crops. Dense green jungles of the stuff thrived along the edges of the road. I had not seen marijuana plants like these since I was at college, although these were certainly a lot bigger and healthier than the ones which graced many a student window-sill. Drug enforcement must be an elusive dream for the local police trying to do their jobs in a county where illegal narcotics can be gathered by the armful without even bothering to get out of the car. On the positive side there would not be too many problems with drug pushers. It would be like trying to sell stinging nettles or thistle leaves in my local pub in Buckinghamshire.

We stopped mid-morning for a rest. I let the horses graze. Roland ignored the dope, Rocky took an experimental mouthful and declared it inedible. He turned his attention to the abundant grass – real grass that is.

It was still morning when we passed through a village called Fostoria. There were lots of trailer houses – nothing more than big caravans – and quite a few real houses, maybe sixty or seventy. Some were in good repair but most were on their way downhill. Fast. There was a small row of boarded-up and thoroughly run-down shops. They were the false-fronted variety seen in western films where the gable end has been squared off with a large planked section that carries the name of the store. The roofs make ideal places for highly expendable badmen to hide with a rifle while waiting to take a pot-shot at the hero of the celluloid range when he rides into town. Of course such third-rate baddies meet their end in the early part of the final shoot-out. Despite receiving a shot clean in the middle of the chest, they are able to defy all the laws of physics and probability by falling forwards off the roof to land in a hay cart parked thoughtfully in front of the store.

I could see that Fostoria had once had quite a thriving business community. There was a garage which had half a dozen very old cars outside. One of the locals told me that it had stopped selling petrol last year because of new government regulations requiring gasoline tanks to be buried underground. Now the inhabitants had to drive ten miles to the nearest gas station – a twenty-mile round trip. They would burn a gallon and a half of fuel just going to fill up.

It was a Sunday and I could hear the congregation singing in the church. I decided to stop and rest the horses for a while. I tied Rocky and Roland to a big white road sign, leaving their lead ropes long so that they could make the best of the belly-high grass.

The sign was built like a goal post with a big white plank forming the crossbar. It pointed the way to Spring Creek Road. The uprights had smaller planks nailed to them. Each bore the name of one of the families which lived along the road and the distance to their house. There were about twenty names in all along a fifteen-mile stretch of road. Four Budenbenders seemed to live within a mile of each other. Elmo Stadel and Roy Stadel were near neighbours. There were some Feists and some Boudreaux, some Lundbergs. Then there were some British names as well: Cox, Williams, Johnston and Jones. One of the Johnstons was called Leroy. Fostoria must have been an interesting place a hundred years ago when all these people from different cultures came together to do business, to celebrate or to marry.

My ruminations were brought to an abrupt halt by the discovery that I had chosen the territory of an ants' nest in which to sit. I got rapidly to my feet and stomped around the road for a moment or two while trying to remove the more ambitious members of the colony from deep within my clothing. Rocky stopped eating to watch my little dance. An elderly lady stood looking at me from the safety of her verandah. I decided that we had enjoyed a long enough break, so I went back to the horses to get them ready to move on. I checked Roland's pack and found that he was developing a sore patch where one of the saddle bags was rubbing on his back. I split the pack between the two horses and decided to walk for the next couple of hours. The temperature was rising fast and I felt that it would be better if we shared the work between the three of us.

Spring Creek Road followed the creek and not the compass. It made a wonderful change to travel along a road which did something other than disappear, straight as a die, into the distance. There were bends. Some were gently curving, others quite abrupt. A bend allows views to unfold in front of you, it offers changes of perspective; it may waste time but it makes a journey more interesting. The changing perspectives even took my mind off the ants which were still making the occasional assault on the more intimate parts of my anatomy. I discovered and ejected five more. I doubted that they would ever find their way home to Fostoria.

In a few places, trees cast shadows across the road. It could almost have been Britain – except for the sharp contrasts of colours: the blue of the sky, the dark greens of the trees and the bright dusty whiteness of the dirt road. The shadows looked, and were, cool and dark but it did not pay to linger under them as they offered shelter from the breeze which was keeping the mosquitoes and deer flies away from us. It was a straight choice; the sun, the breeze and no mosquitoes versus shade and botheration. It was no contest. We kept walking.

We passed a huge number of empty houses and abandoned farms. They outnumbered the occupied properties three to one. Most of them were small wooden bungalows surrounded by a few tumbledown buildings. The grass and the marijuana grows fast in Kansas and nature soon takes over. The fierce summer sun peels paint away in two or three years and the rain and humidity come in. Buildings fall apart within a decade of being abandoned. One or two of the houses were quite grand, with big bay windows and balconies on the upper floors. Back east, or further west where there are more people, more opportunities, more jobs, such places would never have been left to rot.

I noticed a tap outside one empty house and went over to see if I could get some water for the horses. I guessed that the house had been empty for no more than a couple of years. A pair of boots, a serviceable sofa and a wooden box of preserving jars had been left on the verandah. A children's poster of the alphabet using characters from Walt Disney films to illustrate the letters was stuck to the back of the kitchen door.

The tap did not work – no electricity to pump the water up from the well. The sheds were full of old crop spray cans, sacks and broken farm tools. I opened the door of one shed and found that it contained a brand-new sports car covered with a dirty grey tarpaulin. It must have been there for at least a month because there were no signs of any wheel marks in the grass in front of the building. I decided that whoever put the car there had their own reasons for hiding it and would probably resent sharing the knowledge of its existence with a stranger. I left faster than I arrived.

My map showed a large reservoir stretching thirty miles or so along the length of the Big Blue river. I could see none of it – just fields of waving wheat stretching down to the cottonwood-lined banks of the river a couple of miles to the west of us. The second mystery of the afternoon.

As I passed the many streams there would often be a plop or two as turtles which had been sunning themselves on the banks dived into the safety of the water. I noticed a load of smaller birds mobbing a hawk with a red flash on its tail.

My map showed that I was approaching the last house on the road before a gap of four or five miles. I hoped that it would be occupied, otherwise I would have to carry on for another couple of hours before finding somewhere to get water for me and the horses. The house, a tiny single-storey one, was hidden among the trees in a pleasant shady spot. Two small mongrels barked laconically as we approached. There seemed to be a huge number of cats around the place, and a few chickens.

I tied the horses to a fence and knocked on the side of the door frame. An old grey-haired lady peered at me through the fly screen before pushing it open. I asked if I could have some water from the tap in the yard and whether it would be all right to tether the horses in the long grass along the road for the night. She said she thought that it would be fine, in fact she thought it would be quite useful to have the horses graze the grass around the trees on the edge of her property. Mrs Jones told me that I could put my tent in the garden. Her husband would be home soon.

I had just got the horses unloaded and was making a start on pitching the tent when a big black diesel pick-up tickered into the yard. Paul Jones eased himself out of the truck and walked towards me with the rolling gait of a man who needs a new hip. He was wearing a bright shirt and bib and brace overalls. His legs may have been letting him down but Paul had the lively mind and firm handshake of a man half his seventy years. He offered me a bale of hay for the horses. I pointed out that his wife wanted them to graze the grass down around the trees but Paul said that the horses would be better off with the hay.

Paul offered me the use of a shower and his wife produced a massive beef stew with huge lumps of meat and thick greasy gravy. After supper Paul went to get changed and emerged wearing an even brighter shirt and a smart pinstripe bib and brace overall. I tried to do the washing up but Mrs Jones would hear nothing of it. She was insulted that I had actually gone over to make a start at the sink – I am not sure that the new man has penetrated as far as the farms along the banks of the Big Blue river. Paul and I went out to sit on the garden seat to watch the sun go down. As we sat, his two dogs lay dozing at our feet and the cats hunted in the long grass around the edge of the garden. Rocky and Roland stood under their trees winding long twists of hay into their mouths. It was a good way to end the day.

Paul Jones had a deep, quiet voice. A kind voice, tailor-made for listening to. The insects buzzed and the birds sang as he answered my short questions with long answers. I asked him how a man called Jones finished farming the fertile flood plain of the Big Blue river.

His grandfather was a merchant seaman from Bangor, in North Wales. In the 1860s his ship called into New Orleans, where the young Jones saw and smelled the slave ships being unloaded. He went to an auction where sixteen-year-old negro boys changed hands for a thousand dollars apiece. Jones jumped ship and headed north to join the Union army in the hope of helping to put an end to the disgusting trade. His passion was fired by the thought that much of the slave trade was being carried out in British-financed ships manned by British crews. Britain had forsworn slavery a hundred years earlier but she was still a major financial backer of the breakaway Confederate States. British cotton mills were dependent on American cotton, and it was cotton goods from English mills which under-pinned the economic ties between Britain and India. It made good financial sense to ship raw cotton to England and military supplies back to the Confederate States. The British government was keen to see America split into two competing nations – a truly United States would pose a threat to British naval and global supremacy.

'My grandfather served right through the war, then after it was over he started working for a man called Sage – a storekeeper. Well heeled by all accounts. He married his daughter. In 1870 he came out here, looked the place over, bought a farm. Went back to St Louis and he and his wife drove two wagons the 450 miles from Missouri to here. They brought 36,000 dollars-worth of gold with them and bought out forty-two homesteads.'

Paul told me that this area had been divided up into homesteads during the 1860s. Each family was allocated 160 acres of land, a block a quarter of a mile square, and if the family could stay there and improve the property it became theirs to sell.

'Basically the government was betting you 160 acres of land that you could not stay there without starving to death. By the time my grandfather turned up with his bag of gold those first homesteaders were willing to pack up and move on. Some of that land was mighty thin . . . and so were the people living there,' said Paul.

Grandfather Jones settled down to producing nine kids, who settled around the Big Blue. Grandfather Jones's generous father-in-law, whom Paul referred to as Granpa Sage, died in 1900 and left ten thousand dollars to each of his grandchildren.

I asked Paul where Granpa Sage got all his money.

'I don't know where he got it, but they called him a kerbstone banker. He would go to town, sit on the kerb and loan people money.'

'He was a loan shark,' I said.

'I guess you could call him that. Claimed he loaned a lot of money and never lost any.'

Old man Sage made sure that the Jones dynasty of Marshal County got off to a good start, even though it did not carry his name. The Joneses applied themselves with vigour to the business of procreation. Paul said he had twenty-eight cousins and they all had kids and grand-kids.

At one time there were more than twenty Jones families farming in Marshal County. It must have been hard for the book-keepers in Fostoria to make sure that the right Jones was billed for the right goods.

Now there are only two farmer Joneses in the County. And that is a reflection of something which is happening all over the mid-west. Paul told me that Marshal County is a block of land twenty-four miles by twenty-four miles. In 1900 it was home to 24,000 people. Now the population is down to 11,000 and still falling. More and more are squeezed off the land by the fatal combination of more efficient machinery and the occasional farming recession. Those farms which remain grow bigger at about the same speed as their bank overdrafts. This makes them ripe to fall the next time the screws are turned.

'Where have all those people gone now ?' I asked.

'Oh, west most of them,' said Paul. 'That old Oregon Trail is still clogged full of people heading west. They don't use wagons no more, they hire trucks and trailers from U Haul, but they still load them up with all the junk they can carry and leave their past behind them.'

Paul told me about some of the houses I had passed on the way. One breaks his heart to see. He said that the lady who lived there kept the place as neat as could be: 'You could see your face in the polish on the floor.' Her menfolk never wore their shoes in her house. Now the cold Kansas wind blows snow in through the windows. Her once perfect floor is unsafe to walk on.

'Pretty soon, someone will take a bulldozer to it.'

He was quiet for a while, then he pointed to a wren working her way along the side of the garden. She looked like an ordinary British wren to me. He said that he put a nesting box in the garden for her. She and her hyperactive mate come back each spring.

'Those old sticks from last year's nest come a flyin' out of the box. The next day there they are packin' them all back in again. It's my favourite bird. They sing and sing and sing. Hard to believe that liddle biddy bird can produce all that noise – and flies all the way south in the winter. Some claim they bum a ride on top of a duck.'

'Do you believe that?'

'I don't know,' he said with a smile. 'Believe everything you hear and half of what you see.' His smile broadened even more when he realised how he had mashed the proverb.

That evening Paul took me out in his truck to show me a few of the holes in the ground which were home to the early settlers of Marshal County. They had nothing at all save the land, a few hand-tools and the strength of character to hang on until the government handed them the title to the property.

We drove up to a hill where twenty soldiers were massacred by Indians, 'some time in the 1800s' Paul said with the sort of imprecision which would make a historian wince. Their graves were no more than a few scattered piles of stones on top of a hill which is now a cattle pasture. At least the markers on the soldiers' graves had lasted a hundred years. The corpses of the Indians had been left out in the open for the coyotes and crows to clear away. Paul said that when the Indians win it is called a massacre, when the whites win it is called a battle. I thought that Paul Jones had inherited more than land from his Grandpa Jones who had jumped ship to fight for the abolition of slavery.

Then I spoiled it all by asking about the non-existent Tuttle Creek Lake which appeared deep and blue on the maps but which was invisible from the ground. He told me that it was just an occasional lake – part of a flood control scheme. He waved his arm towards the Big Blue river. When the rains were heavy they closed the gates and held the river until it backed up right to within thirty feet of Paul's front door. The land was farmed in the knowledge that once every ten years it would rain hard enough to justify flooding the valley. The scheme was designed to prevent a repeat of the terrible flooding which struck Kansas City in the 1950s and which claimed so many lives in the black quarters of the city.

'Moved whole towns to protect them damn city niggers,' said Paul.

As we stood and looked at the last of the day disappearing into the west I wondered whether Grandfather Jones would have approved of such sentiments and such language.

7

Hickok, cock-up and public relations

We crossed into Nebraska. It looked pretty much the same as Kansas. The wildlife was pretty much the same as well – except there was probably more of it, especially the type of wildlife which always comes to find you: insects. I used to hate English flies. They spit on your food, leave little black full-stops as evidence of their passage and generally buzz around in a most infuriating fashion. This is civilised behaviour compared to that of their American cousins. Prairie flies do all of the above – and then they eat you. I could not believe it when I felt a sharp stabbing pain in my arm and looked down to see an innocuous fly quietly munching away at my skin. It was eating me through my shirt.

God has also blessed America with one of his more vicious creations – deer flies. They are about a third of an inch long with delicate blue-grey, slightly translucent wings which fold back like the foils of a jet fighter. They are sometimes referred to as B52s because of their habit of flying high overhead – well above antler height – choosing their target area and then making a sudden and rapid dive. Stukas would be a better name. They are highly selective in their targeting – they are the 'smart' bombers of the insect world. They left Rocky completely alone but maintained a frenzied attack on Roland and me for most of the trip across the prairies.

Then there are the mosquitoes. British mosquitoes have

the decency to go to bed at lunchtime and leave you in peace for at least a few hours during the day. Nebraskan mosquitoes really suck. Me mostly. The trouble with travelling with horses is that you are broadcasting to all flesh-eating insects within a three-mile radius that warm, fresh blood is available. To a mosquito or deer fly a horse is a giant 'Eat Here' sign. I was travelling with two horses. The flies, mosquitoes and other flesh-eaters home in on the smell of the horses and then find something far nicer to eat – an Englishman.

It was incredible. We would be travelling along a dirt road scything across thousands of acres of wall-to-wall corn fields which had been sprayed to wildlife sterility by pesticides – and the insects would come to find us. The horses and I must have been the only living warm-blooded animals within miles and we had our own ravenous aerial cortège.

I spent a long time looking for a cheerful side to our predicament. I eventually found one. If there were so many insects patrolling our particular piece of nowhere, then there must be an awful lot of mosquitoes which die a slow, hungry death because they were not lucky enough to bumble across three succulent travellers.

Even more unpleasant horrors lurk in every patch of grass to the east of the Rockies. These are chiggers. I cannot describe one because I never saw one. They are too small to be seen with the naked eye. They live in the grass and wait for something to come past – me. They jump, squirm, hop, or even slither for all I know, from the grass on to the bottom of your trousers. They then find some flesh. But chiggers are discerning consumers. Not for them the horny skin of ankle or foot. They start climbing north until they find a nice warm soft fleshy part – usually between three and four feet above ground level. It is there that they take up residence, or lay their eggs, or merely stop for a drink. Whatever it is they do there, the end result is an itchy, an incredibly itchy, red blotch which stays for several days. Had I not been celibate during my trip through the prairies I would have assumed that I had picked up some awful sexually transmitted disease.

I hoped to spend my first night in Nebraska at the Rock Creek Pony Express station, which used to be a major stopping point on the Oregon Trail. An entrepreneur called Dave McCanles built a bridge across Rock Creek. For the wagon trains it was a case of use McCanles bridge or dig a cutting on both sides of the river bank. McCanles charged what he thought the wagons could afford – everyone paid up.

The park superintendent said that we were welcome to stay. He offered the horses a corall which was knee-deep in beautiful fresh grass and said that I could sleep in a replica log cabin which had been built on the site of the old Pony Express station. Wayne loaned me a couple of books about the place and I stayed up well into the night reading them. It was wonderful to be able to sit up at a table to read rather than crouch in the tent like an animal. It felt like home with my own room, bed, table and bench. Admittedly the bench was hard, the bed had no mattress, there was no glass in the window, I was reading by candlelight, the nearest toilet and drinkable water was half a mile away, and the room was full of mosquitoes. A few weeks earlier I would have considered these to be pretty rough living conditions – now they seemed positively luxurious. The best thing was being able to do my cooking on the table rather than having to squat down on the floor. Even putting my trousers on without having to squirm around in the confines of the tent seemed wonderful.

As I sat there reading by candlelight I could hear the local coyotes howling and yipping their messages to each other. Their voices soar up and down through the scales. Sometimes it will be a solo effort, then a whole pack will join in, then another and another, until the air is filled with their screams and whoops. The noise makes my skin crawl. It is hard to believe that they are dogs.

Rock Creek Station, Nebraska, is famous for two things: a murdering philanderer called Hickok who managed to portray himself as a hero, and a financial disaster which became glorified as the Pony Express. Hickok has gone down in history as one of the brave, gun-happy heroes who helped to carve a civilisation out of the 'Wild West', and the Pony Express is perceived as uniting a nation split in half by geography. Both are prime examples of America's greatest gift to the world – public relations. Even a hundred years ago the Americans were beginning to show real promise at this most corrupting of skills.

The Pony Express was a financial disaster on a magnificent scale. The timing was wrong, the idea was wrong and the market for its services was truly minuscule and short-lived. There were two competing routes for the coast to coast stage coach. One swung south out of the worst of the weather. The other, shorter, more northerly route was considered to be much more dangerous. The Pony Express was established to prove that the northerly route was best. Within eighteen months of its establishment the telegraph wires had reached the coast and the three main investors – Waddell, Russell and Majors – had lost their shirts.

Wild Bill Hickok was also tied up with the Pony Express. He was a stable boy. The people who work at Rock Creek Station today are convinced that he was a cold-blooded murderer. The story is that Dave McCanles went to the Pony Express Station to collect money which was owed to him, taking two friends and his twelve-year-old son with him. None of them was armed. The station manager was a man called Horace Wellman. No one knows the precise circumstances of the ensuing fracas save that Bill Hickok was in one of the cabins with someone else's wife and he fired the first shot from his position in the bedroom.

McCanles's companions were shot and wounded as they tried to run off. They were then clubbed to death down by the river. McCanles's twelve-year-old son escaped. Hickok and Wellman were charged with murder but were acquitted.

One other piece of information is that Wild Bill Hickok was often called 'Duck Bill' because of the size of his nose. A man can easily lose his temper if someone is foolish enough to insult him in front of his lady friend.

The two oxen which are used to offer wagon rides to the public at Rock Creek station are called Bill and Dave in memory of Hickock and McCanles. Bill is a bully. These massive beasts are rather difficult to deal with. They have massive five-foot horn spans and can kick in almost any direction. When the staff at Rock Creek go out into the field to catch the cattle they take a small green brush with them. The oxen love to be brushed and as soon as they see their brush they will arch their backs ready to be groomed. But if you do not have the brush in your hand then you would do well to watch out for the horns and the hooves.

The oxen walk extremely slowly – a sedate two miles an hour. However, they were the most common draught animals to be found on the trail. They scored on several counts over horses. Oxen can live off terrible food whereas a horse needs quite good feed if it is to stay in working condition. Horses and mules easily get rubbed raw by chafing harnesses, always a problem on the trail, and if the pressure is not removed the sore will go septic. The animal may get blood poisoning and die. Oxen, however, form rough calluses on their hides where yokes or traces rub, which was a huge advantage. They were also preferred because the Indians were not interested in stealing them.

The bull whacker at Rock Creek is a man called Roy Capell and I asked his advice about the problems I might face on the trail. He walked over to a hose-pipe, took his knife out of his pocket and cut me two six-inch lengths. He told me that grazing horses often get bitten on the nose by rattlesnakes. If this happens their noses swell up and their nostrils close. They asphyxiate. He told me to keep the two bits of hose in my kit. If one of my horses got bitten I was to shove the bits of hose up his nose and start praying.

Yes, well.

8

Zigzagging, telepathic grader drivers and accurate expectoration

As the miles scrolled past us, I developed a useful theory about roadside litter and what it could tell about the towns which lay ahead. Boxes, bags and drink-cups from just one of the national hamburger chains meant that the town was home to at least two thousand people but probably less than five thousand. Two or three national chains meant that it was between five and ten thousand. After that the variety and quantity of litter goes up exponentially.

Even more useful information can be gleaned from the size of the discarded soft drinks containers along the side of the road. Americans seem to consume fizzy drinks in unbelievable quantities. Most petrol stations or general stores will have a 'soda fountain' where you can buy a cup marked according to size: 8, 12, 20, 32 and even 40 oz. These giant waxed-paper cartons are given names such as the 'Gulp', the 'Giant Gulp' or the Thirstbuster II'. Forty ounces of fizzy drink is well over two pints. Even allowing for the small ice flow Americans like to add to their drinks, this is still a huge amount of sugary liquid. They will even abuse tea in the same way. It takes a robust constitution and a thoroughly corrupt palate to consume over two pints of ice-cold, sugary, often fizzy, chemical-laden liquid in one session.

As soon as I left a town I would see the more modest-sized containers along the verge. Three miles from town the 20-oz 'Gulps' would start to appear, at four miles the 32-oz 'Giant Gulps' could be found and from five to six miles onwards the 40-oz 'Thirstbusters' would litter the ditches like discarded flowerpots.

I was now trying to swing north-west towards the Platte river and it was getting increasingly hard to find roads which went in the right direction. It was about 130 miles from Rock Creek to Fort Kearny if you could take a direct line. However, Nebraska has been divided up into one-mile sections by a grid system of dirt roads which run due north/south or due east/west. We had to zigzag along thirty miles of dirt roads to make twenty miles of trail. My maps told me exactly where the trail had gone scything through what were now fields of corn. We had to walk around two sides of the triangle.

The gravel roads vary immensely in quality. At their best they are a fine mixture of sand and small stones, offering a perfect blend of grip and give for the horses. They can be just about as good a surface as a horse could ever want. At their worst they are covered in walnut-sized stones and rocks which bash the soft underfoot with every step. When the road is like this the cars and trucks form narrow tracks where the stones have been pushed beneath the surface. The horses would try to find the smoothest part of the road and stick with that.

The locals barrel along the roads at sixty or seventy miles an hour with their cars bucking and jumping across the ruts. Steering joints wear out fast in the mid-west. Wheels need constant realignment. The cars throw a spiralling plume of dust up behind them. The locals never slow down for the crossroads which occur every mile where the section roads meet; they scan the horizon looking for the dust plumes created by traffic coming in from right or left. County roads are dangerous places to be on the first day of rain after a dry spell when the tell-tale dust has been laid. If two vehicles hit the same intersection at sixty miles an hour the result is a bloody mess.

On windless days the dust hangs in the air for minutes after a vehicle has disappeared – like the frozen wake of a boat. But windless days are not common in the prairies. The strong south-westerly breeze picks up the dust and shifts it off in the direction of Quebec. We were always travelling on the north or east side of the road and the dust always came our way. No wonder that the wagon trains would fan out across the prairie to avoid travelling in each other's dust trails. If one truck or car can produce these great plumes of dust, then a wagon train with twenty wagons and two hundred oxen could produce a hideous amount of the stuff. Then there would be the herds of cattle, sheep and horses which travelled with the emigrants. Thousands of hooves making their own contribution to a mobile dust storm. The animals often suffered respiratory problems, some worse than others. Oxen always worked in the same position in the team. And it was the right-hand animals which got the worst of it. They walked along with their heads down in the dust thrown up by their partners. Later emigrants learned to rotate their oxen around the teams, the way modern motorists rotate tyres around their cars.

The Nebraskans were turning out to be much friendlier than I had been led to expect. It is a universal rule that people reserve their best stupidity jokes for their nearest neighbours. New Yorkers tell jokes about Polacks, French about Belgians and Idahoans tell jokes about blonde girls, but then they also have 'Famous Potatoes' on their car tax plates. Kansans tell jokes at the expense of their Nebraskan neighbours. Kansans believe that Nebraska is a flat, boring country filled with flat, boring people. Which is pretty rich coming from people who live in a state that makes Lincolnshire seem geographically fascinating. I had been in

Nebraska for six days and it was no flatter and no more boring than Kansas – although the Nebraskans had come up trumps on the hospitality stakes. Since crossing the border my tent had stayed in its bag – I had been offered accommodation at every place that I stopped.

The Nebraskans also seemed more curious than their near neighbours in Kansas. Several times a day trucks or cars would stop and the driver would make polite enquiries about my trip. Most of them seemed to be close relatives of the last one to stop. It was nice to have people to talk to, although at times the inquisition seemed slightly less than polite. It was always the old men in pick-ups whose manner was most unsettling.

They would usually drive past once, then come back the other way at a lower speed. They would pull up at the third pass – bathing the three of us in dust on each occasion. As the cloud cleared away to the east, the truck window would start to descend. As it came, a big blob of saliva, rendered brown and gelatinous by tobacco juice, would come flying out. The amorphous gobbet of juice would miss the top of the window by a hair and splat land on the parched road surface. The gradual descent of the window would continue. As it approached the end of its run a grubby elbow would emerge from the darkness of the truck to force it down the last few inches to total immersion in the Detroit-built door frame. With these guys it was always Ford or Chevy, never a Japanese job – memories are too long and too vivid in the mid-west. Then a brown face, wrinkled and dried by half a century of prairie sun and wind, would appear. A straw hat would be pushed back to reveal an incongruously white and crevasse-free forehead.

The tobacco would make a few more rounds of the mouth before being parked up between lip and gum where it would be almost, but not quite, out of the way of conversation. Then came the summons, accompanied by the faintest wag of a finger.

'Over here.'

These guys were old enough to have been around when horses were still the main form of transport. Old enough to know that it was only poor people or idiots who rode horses for travelling. Better off people drove pick-up trucks. The travelling man on the horse was almost the lowest form of human life.

I was rather angry and confused by the first two or three of these encounters but I soon began to take pleasure in their predictability. I would meekly move the horses closer to the truck. The tobacco would drop back into play between teeth and tongue as an unhurried and practised eye assessed us; horses first, then me.

Another gob of juice would be liberated. Then: 'Where have you come from then, fella?'

'I am from England but we started out from Kansas City.' A think, a chew, a forehead rub.

'And where you headed to then, fella?'

'Oregon.'

The answer would give rise to a long pause as the information went in and more tobacco juice came out – usually to land in exactly the same brown stain where the other two gobbets had fetched up. A man can take pride in the accuracy of expectorating.

I waited patiently, savouring the moment while the concept fermented in the grey cells. It could take as long as thirty seconds of ruminating but the response always came. It was usually delivered more by way of an offer of information than an exclamation.

'Well that's a heck of a long ways to go.'

It came out as though I was such an idiot that I was not aware that Oregon was two whole states away rather than just in the next county – as though I did not know the meaning of another 1,500 miles of horseback riding.

Sometimes that would be virtually the end of the conversation. I might get nothing more than being wished good luck on my trip. At other times a longer discussion might follow and a suggestion might be made about somewhere to stay or even a firm offer of accommodation for me and the horses. I asked one old boy, who was minded to stop and talk at the side of the road, why the Nebraskans were so kind to strangers – especially passing horsemen.

Bill leaned his back against his truck and explained that there were two ways of looking at the situation – one true, one not so true.

'This is a big country. More than a day's ride between towns. People always offered hospitality to strangers – a full belly and a dry place to sleep. You never knew when you might have to set off across country yourself and then it would be your turn to benefit from the system.

'Besides, in them days travelling horsemen were the only source of news. They would stop and talk. If their talk was good and their stories tall enough then they would be invited to share supper with the family. If it was really good then the neighbours might come around as well.'

It seemed a recipe for embellishing and even inventing stories of the outside world.

'I guess that's right,' said Bill, and he offered me a swig from a dirty one-gallon flask which was propped upright amongst the junk in the back of his pick-up. I could feel ice slopping around as I hefted it to my lips. It was water rather than the sweet iced tea favoured by Nebraska farmers.

'Then of course there is the idea that people offered hospitality to strangers to help them on their way out of the county. Not to offer might have prompted some stealing. Even bad men find it hard to steal from people who have been kind to them. And it might be better to have the guy sleeping in the barn where you know where he is rather than sneaking into the yard at night.'

I asked Bill which of his explanations was true, mutual co-operation or fear. His face cracked with a smile and he winked.

We shook hands. Bill eased his buttocks back into the permanent dip on the driver's side of his truck seat and drove off. I lifted the horses' heads from the long grass at the side of the road, climbed up on to Roland and turned my attention to carrying on west.

The dirt roads are cheap to build but quite expensive to maintain. Every time a car or truck passes along the road stones and other lighter material are thrown over to the outer edges. After a month or so the centre of the road becomes beautifully smooth and slightly dish-shaped. The locals can then drive even faster on this smooth surface, which keeps them in the middle of the road. This would be fine as long as it never rained. But any moisture collects in this giant rut and half an inch of rain turns the dished surface into a quagmire.

A grading machine comes along once a month and pushes all the debris back into the middle of the road. This keeps a proper crown on the road so that the rain runs off. But the grader brings all sorts of rubble back into the middle of the road and makes driving extremely difficult. The locals have to drive at forty miles an hour instead of their usual seventy. Everyone hates the grader driver. Of course there are times when it rains so hard that even the best-shaped dirt roads are reduced to mud and no one can get along them. Then everyone hates the grader driver even more. The poor man is about as popular as a traffic warden.

In the old days the road graders were huge steel blades pulled by teams of twenty or thirty horses. Now all that power is crammed under the bonnet of six-wheel monsters built by John Deere or Caterpillar. The cab, engine and transmission are at the back of the machine while the front wheels are stuck well out ahead on the end of two long steel beams. The grading blade is tucked neatly away under the machine. They have the look of a giant mechanical praying mantis.

The grader drivers patrol their patch of Nebraska, tending and mothering their bits of road. Their reward for this essential and lonely task is a steady but unexciting salary and the contempt of all their neighbours. Nearly every farmer I met described his local grader operator as a 'complete asshole'. Most of them claimed to know a monkey who could do a better job. The lonely grader drivers talk to each other on their radios and will often meet up to share their packed lunches where their territories meet. During the winter the grading blade is removed and a snow plough is bolted on in its place. Then the grader drivers become everybody's hero. It is they who keep the snow off the roads and who allow the farmers access to the outside world. Then they can get to the café where they can have a good moan about the grader driver.

For a while in Nebraska I got hooked into a chain of grader operators. They passed me on from one to the other, finding me places to stay and checking up on my progress. They would turn up out of the blue, knowing my name, my horses and even the name of my wife. They would sometimes turn up with extra food or a cold drink for me. Sometimes a car would stop and it would be a road grader's wife – who also seemed to know all about me. I started to look forward to seeing one of the giant machines on the horizon, travelling along in the centre of its own dust cloud, though it was disconcerting telling an anecdote to a man I had never met, only for him to tell me that he had already heard it over the radio from the man I had met the day before. The next day I would meet another grader driver and carry on with what was essentially the same conversation. I was beginning to feel like the only non-telepath in Nebraska.

We stayed with one grader driver who owned a big friendly hairy mongrel called Kujo. I was rather flattered because the dog slept right beside my tent all night. When I woke up in the morning, I discovered that he had eaten all my supplies of beef jerky, my granola bars and most of my dried fruit. If there was any justice in the world he should have been as sick as I felt. Kujo had clearly fallen in love with my saddle pack and the next morning he started following me up the road. His owner told me that he would soon give up and come home.

Initially I was glad of the company. Rocky and Roland had heard all my jokes. Kujo smiled politely at them and wagged his tail every time I talked to him. Dogs are much better company than horses. But after five miles I was beginning to think that it was time for Kujo to head off home so I decided that I had better stop talking to him altogether. He stayed right there with us, trotting along beside Rocky. For some reason he had decided not to trust Roland. Besides, Rocky had the pack saddle that day. Then I told him to go home. He just backed off a bit but kept on coming. I turned the horses around and walked them back east, telling Kujo to 'go away'. He stayed. So I tried out some of my new American vocabulary on him, No good, he just stayed twenty-five yards away down the road. He started following us again as soon as I wheeled the horses back towards the west.

Then I got off and picked up a handful of stones and lobbed a few in his direction – aiming to miss. It had no effect. So I lobbed a few more – aiming to hit. An unbiased observer would have been hard pushed to detect a change in strategy. Kujo was a canny dog and worked out just how far I could throw a stone. He backed out of range and stayed there.

I did not know what to do next. So I stopped for lunch. Kujo watched hopefully. Then I saw a plume of dust and along came another road grader. I started to tell my story to the driver but he seemed to know more about me than I did. He knew that Kujo was with me and told me that he had already arranged for someone to come and pick him up.

I felt that I was beginning to lose control of my own life, as though there was some unseen force co-ordinating my whole trip. It was rather nice after having felt alone for so long.

9

A Mexican showdown, a gallery of plasters and seeing the elephant

The horses and I were settling down to a routine. We were making a steady twenty miles a day. I had given up the attempt to teach Roland to walk faster but Rocky had slowed down to match paces. At least they were now travelling at the same speed. My aim was to be up and about by 5.30 a.m. and on the road by 7.30. We would travel for a couple of hours, take a twenty-minute break and then carry on until 11.30 when we would stop for lunch – usually near a house where I could get some water. The plan was to hit the road again at 1.30 or so. I would then start looking for somewhere to stay soon after 3.00. This routine meant that we were travelling through the hottest part of the day but I could not see any way around that – not if I was going to avoid turning up at someone's house late in the evening.

The horses were extremely fit and my worries about them losing weight during the trip had proved unfounded. I had been able to get plenty of grain for them and the grass had been first-rate all along the trail. Most nights I had found a field to turn them into but occasionally I had to tether them on long ropes to graze a circle of grass around a peg. Then I had to keep a careful watch. Roland would get himself tied up in knots with the tether. He would panic and kick out, giving himself nasty rope burns on his legs.

Rocky was much more adept. He seldom got himself into trouble with the tether. But he was worrying me in other ways. His feet were not as good as they could have been. He had had new shoes fitted just before I left Independence in Missouri and twice since then he had needed the attention of a blacksmith because his shoes kept on working loose. The trouble was that his feet were starting to dry out in the heat and he was developing some unpleasant cracks in them. He was not in any pain but he really needed time to grow some more hoof before someone else tried to drive yet another set of nails up into his feet. I was starting to walk a lot more to try to keep the pressure off him. If he lost a shoe the cracks in his feet would really start to grow and then he would have to stop and rest for quite a few weeks. If I could catch up with the wagon train then I could throw part of my pack into one of their support vehicles, which would allow me to take even more pressure off him.

I asked nearly everyone I met if they had seen anything of the wagon train but no one could tell me how far behind them I really was. Some said a few days, others put it as far as three weeks ahead of me. I hoped that it would not be as much as that. Closing a three-week gap would be impossible – especially with a horse with bad feet.

One afternoon I stopped at a farm for water. A lady came out to see me and we talked for a while. She asked me how my trip was going. I told her that everything was fine except that horses are not the world's greatest travelling companions. I said that by the end of the first week I was talking to myself, by the end of week two I was talking to the horses as though they were old friends. It was about week three that they started talking back to me. Then, at the end of the first month, I was lying in my tent one night when I heard the horses talking about me behind my back.

'Clearly I must have been going mad. I mean I would never normally have listened in on another conversation,' I said. It was a little joke which usually went down quite well. I looked into her face and saw only sympathy for my mental plight.

She then showed me a cattle trough in a corner of the yard. I walked the horses over and found the trough surrounded by pig manure. I gingerly walked through it. The horses had buried their heads gratefully in the trough when another horse suddenly appeared on the other side of the fence – he was running at full pelt. Roland lifted his head, swung around and started to run. Rocky followed suit. I was too stupid to let go of the lead ropes and got dragged backwards through the pig manure. It had been ripening nicely in the Nebraskan sun. I was smeared from head to foot but the horses did not get away.

I looked over at the lady and expected to see her laughing but that look of pity had come right back. I decided that I did not stand much chance of getting anywhere else to stay that day, smelling and looking the way that I did then, so I asked if I could pitch my tent in her yard. She offered to wash my clothes for me. I was extremely grateful. My next major target was Fort Kearny which is where the trail joins the Platte river. We would then be following this laconic slug of a river for the next four or five hundred miles – right through to Casper – almost half way across Wyoming.

The emigrants were quite dismissive of the silt-laden Platte river. One described it as being 'too thick to drink and too thin to plough'. It had the reputation of being a dirty, lazy gipsy of a river. It would mess up its own bed by filling it with silt collected from the Rockies. It would then move off elsewhere, shifting a few hundred yards, or even miles, further north or south. On occasions the Platte would fall out with itself and divide into two channels, leaving immense lozenges of land where trees could thrive protected from the annual prairie fires. For the emigrants it offered the welcome sight of the first decent trees since leaving the Missouri.

It was a Friday afternoon as I stumbled the last few miles

to Fort Kearny. I had promised myself two days off at the state camp ground where I knew there were showers and facilities for washing my clothes.

Unfortunately the dirt roads passed through a series of sand hills which stood between us and the Platte river. These had once been sand dunes thrown up by the winds from the great American desert. They were now covered with a thin patina of top soil which offered good grazing in the spring but nothing worth eating for the rest of the year. The road had been bulldozed through the hills, cutting away the top soil to reveal a granular sand underneath. It was like walking through a bowl of sugar. Walking was hard for all three of us. I must have looked like a ham actor as I did the desert stagger through the sand, which held my feet and filled my shoes. I longed to climb up on to Rocky's back and let him do the work but I convinced myself that when we got to the top of the next hill the Platte river would be sparkling in the distance. The sand hills are small, three rises and dips per mile. Three times an hour I hoped I would see the river and three times an hour I stood waist-deep in disappointment contemplating the next dip and rise rather than the longed for view of the river.

Finally, at about four in the afternoon, I breasted a hill to see a dark green line of cottonwood trees – always a welcome sign of water. I could not actually see the river but the trees were as good as the sight of sun shining off water. The road surface started to firm up as we came down from the hills and on to the rich silty flood-plain farmland which was all that stood between me and the end of a hard day.

My sand road joined the tarmac highway running in front of the Fort Kearny State Historical Park and I saw a buff-coloured Nebraska Parks Service pick-up truck coming towards me. I waved and jumped up and down to attract the driver's attention but he drove straight on past. I stopped waving thinking that he had failed to spot me but he swung the truck around in a U-turn and came back.

Park Trooper Joe told me that I and the horses were welcome to stay for a few days and he directed me to a place where I could pitch my tent and told me where there was a field for the horses. He mentioned that his wife was away and asked if I wanted to join him at the Mexican restaurant in town. It sounded marvellous as I had been eating my dried food for the previous three or four days.

'Just a mile to go,' he said, as though it was not far. For us it was another twenty minutes' walking.

I led the horses in through the main gate of the camp ground. I think I was hobbling slightly as I walked. The student on duty at the gate had already been warned by Joe that I was coming and he asked me if I had really come all the way from Kansas City. I told him that I had.

'And you are going on to Oregon,' he said.

'That is my plan,' I said, not feeling able to commit myself to anything more definite.

I followed the tarmac road which wound through the camp ground with its many small lakes and large cotton-wood trees. Nearly every pitch was occupied by the massive plastic palaces which pass for touring caravans in the United States. Most of them have carport-sized awnings jutting out from the side where their proud proprietors sit on sun loungers to smoke and drink and occasionally stir them-selves to prod the ceiling-tile-sized steaks which sizzle on the barbecues. The idea seems to be to live a little of the small town existence, to sit out the evening on the front stoop and watch the world go by. That evening they had me to look at.

The blue, meat-juice-laden smoke from the barbecues curled upwards to mix with the drifting wisps of white fluff coming down from the cottonwood trees. There was a sense of unreality about the whole thing as I led Rocky and Roland through the full but strangely quiet camp site. Some of the rigs were thirty feet in length, more like mobile homes than mere caravans. Many had air-conditioning units humming quietly on their roofs. It seemed to me that Americans had the sensible idea about how to see their country. It had been designed by God to be viewed at fifty miles an hour rolling past the windows of an air-conditioned truck. I felt like a time-traveller thrown a hundred years into the future. The campers watched me come, much as you might imagine a stranger would be analysed as he came into a real western town. Americans are usually friendly people but I suppose that I looked such an unlikely sight, a man walking with two well-laden horses, that they just watched us go by. Something to think on and talk about that evening.

I found the field for the horses, offered them water and then checked their feet. A few of the splits on Rocky's hooves had moved on beyond the lines I had marked to check their progress. Despite the hoof dressing and my efforts to take the pressure off by walking rather than riding, his feet were getting worse every day. He was not yet lame but it could not be long before the splits penetrated to the quick – then we would be in trouble. I turned the horses free to bury their heads in the tall grass, to flick tails and stomp feet at the persistent mosquitoes of the Platte river.

I erected the tent and then hobbled over to the wash-rooms to strip the gallery of plasters I had stuck all over my damaged feet and to take a long, slow, skin-wrinkling shower. My hobble was even more pronounced as I made my way back to the tent. I sat at a picnic table to examine the state of my feet and counted fifteen blisters, although it was hard to be accurate as there were several which over-lapped. I confess to extracting a certain amount of masoch-istic pleasure from my end-of-day blister inspection. Blisters are tangible evidence of the effort I had put into my walking. They had two days to recover – it would not really be enough. My feet were not in much better condition than Rocky's. Of the three of us, Roland was the only one who was really fit for the road.

That evening Park Trooper Joe took me across the river to the town of Kearny. Mexican restaurants are to America what Indian restaurants are to Britain – places where the working man can get a good meal out for a reasonable price. They are also places where the unwise or unwary can systematically annihilate their taste-buds. The items on the menu were completely alien to me, so I told Joe that I would have whatever he had. He warned me that it might be too hot for me but I told him that I had enjoyed several years of intensive training on hot food in Indian restaurants. I had to explain that I meant Asian Indian food, not American Indian food. Anything the Mexicans can cook up, the Indians can do hotter.

The gauntlet had been thrown down and I had been foolish enough to pick it up. Joe guided us through the menu. Each dish and choice got hotter and hotter as we went. I matched him sauce for sauce, jalapino for jalapino. He watched me carefully, seeking signs of weakness. It was like a game of poker. I did my best to prevent the fire in my throat showing through to my expression. I sipped my beer while thinking that I would rather be dunking my whole head in the pitcher of iced water. But the honour of nations was at stake. To have shown signs of gastronomic weakness would have been to concede defeat. I think I acquitted myself well – but without much dignity.

That night I lay in the tent wondering if Joe's alimentary canal felt in better shape than mine – I hoped not.

Fort Kearny had been built in 1849 and today's State Historical Park with its huge camp site includes a full-size replica stockade plus a visitors' centre. For a long time after the opening of the Oregon Trail, the fort was the last outpost of American government authority the emigrants would see until they got clear to Oregon. From here on in they were on their own. This was their last chance to pack up and go home with their tail between their legs.

Government freighters came out this far to bring supplies to Fort Kearny. The emigrants who decided that they had had enough could sell their wagons and animals to other emigrants at fairly good prices and get a ride back east in one of the returning freight wagons. They had a phrase for giving up. They called it 'seeing the elephant'. Basically the emigrants had come up against something which was just too huge, too alien, too far outside their comprehension to overcome. They had decided to throw in the towel.

Many of the emigrants were keen writers of diaries. They knew that they were embarking on a great adventure, something which would change their lives and those of their children and grandchildren. And just as the people and their motives for making the trip varied, so too did the diaries. They range from mere logs, which record the miles made and the deaths along the way, through to full, and possibly rather fanciful, reports of the journey. One thing they all have in common, no matter how rudimentary, is a rather unsettling acceptance of human morbidity and mortality.

One young girl wrote: 'Our mother was taken about two o'clock this morning with a violent diarrhoea attended with cramps. She, however, aroused no one until daylight when everything was done which we possibly could to save her life, but her constitution long impaired by disease was unable to withstand the attack.'

About one in ten died, some thirty thousand in all. Hollywood would have us believe that most of those deaths were at the hands of the Indians. But though the Indians might have killed four hundred people in the first twenty years of the operation of the trail, they traded with the whites and helped the wagons to get across many of the rivers. They probably saved more lives than they took.

Many people were killed by guns but mostly in accidents. The guns of the day could be discharged merely by being jolted. A moment of carelessness in removing a gun from its scabbard or from its resting place in the back of a wagon could cause the loss of life or limb. Then each day men would be sent out from the wagon train into unfamiliar territory to find game to shoot. Hunting accidents were common.

Then there were accidents connected with the wagons themselves. The emigrants were trying to move all their worldly possessions across half a continent and many of them were totally inexperienced at the specialist job of freighting. They were dealing with huge forces – teams of ten or twelve oxen and 5-ton wagons.

An emigrant called Edwin Bryant wrote: 'A boy eight or nine years old had his leg crushed by falling from the tongue of the wagon and being run over by its wheels.' The family had wrapped the leg in cloth and encased it in a wooden box to try to prevent it from moving while the child was bounced along in the back of the wagon for the next seven days.

Bryant went on: 'In this condition the child had remained without any dressing of his wounded limb, until last night, when he called to his mother that he could feel worms crawling in his leg . . . it was discovered that gangrene had taken place and the limb of the child was swarming with maggots. The child's leg, from his foot to his knee, was in a state of putrefaction.'

But it was disease which took the biggest toll, dysentery, food poisoning and the dreaded cholera. In the early part of the trip the wagon trains stopped to dig proper graves and to give the dead a decent burial but as time pressure increased and deaths became more frequent, arrangements for the dead became more and more rudimentary. As the wagons rolled west they would come across the graves of those who had gone before them. Many had been dug up by coyotes or Indians. It became the custom to wrap the dead in a blanket, bury them in a fairly shallow grave and then the following morning the whole wagon train would drive, one at a time, over the grave in the hope that the confusion of smells and compaction caused by hooves and wheels would put both human and animal grave robbers off their purpose.

The next morning I went over to see to the horses and check them over. Roland's back was looking better and I made a close inspection of Rocky's feet. The greasing that I had begun too late was slowing up the development of the cracks but his back right hoof was in quite a bad state. Only three of the eight shoe nails were doing any good. Two of the cracks on the outer edge of the foot were in danger of joining up. If they did, a chunk of the hoof might come off, the shoe would drop off soon afterwards and then the foot would not have much of a chance to recover. Fortunately the cracks were still well clear of the quick and he was not suffering any pain.

The rate at which horses grow hoof varies a great deal with their nutrition and the amount of exercise they are getting. The more they walk the greater the blood flow through the foot. Rocky's hooves were growing but not fast enough to outrun the cracks. I needed to find a way of giving him some time to rest, which would not be easy without bringing the journey to another halt.

After breakfast I sat at my camp-site picnic table and thought about the future course of my trip. For the first time I had to contemplate failure. I had done between a quarter and a third of the trip. I was failing to achieve my target of a hundred miles a week. I had lost a week when Roland injured Rocky back at Clinton Lake, I had lost three more days at Rock Creek while I rested the horses and it now looked as though Rocky needed more time off. All my problems had been caused by my inability to manage the horses. I should never have turned my back on them while they were feeding and I should have been greasing their feet from the start to stop them from drying out. I was failing to make good progress on what should have been the easy part of the trip.

I thought about the emigrants and wondered whether I had seen the elephant. Certainly I was having problems with my stock and I was not in the best of health. My feet were a mess and my bowels were in some disarray – the latter was my fault.

The previous night Joe had mentioned his state colleagues at the Buffalo Bill Ranch a hundred miles further west along the trail in North Platte, where he said that I would be able to stay. He also mentioned that they make runs back and forth between the two state parks because they share equipment – hole borers, generators and the like. Joe had joked that it would be easy to load the horses and me into the trailer.

'You could be there by mid-day tomorrow,' he said.

I was not ready to cheat that much but I might be prepared to cheat a little. I had walked about 90 of the last 110 miles anyway. I could leave Rocky at Fort Kearny and set off west on foot with all the gear loaded on Roland. Joe had said that they were due to make a trip over to North Platte on Wednesday. They could take Rocky. That would give him the best part of a week off. I could reassess the situation when I got to North Platte.

It was not much of a plan but it would keep me moving west. It was cheating because I would be using modern technology to buy a rest for Rocky but I would still be using muscle power to make the trip.

Joe turned up in his fawn Nebraska State truck. He was grinning as he asked whether I was feeling alright this morning.

I matched him smile for smile and said that I was feeling 'just fine'. I offered him coffee and put the plan to him. Within an hour he had called through to North Platte and everything was fixed up. It was Saturday. Rocky would remain at Fort Kearny until Tuesday or Wednesday when he would be moved to North Platte. I was to take two days off and then start walking west with Roland.

I did not actually see the elephant at Fort Kearny but I think I may have trodden in one or two of his dumps.

10

Dirty Woman Ranch, a polite automaton and salvation in a yellow van

I cut down my equipment as much as possible and left a pile of gear for Joe to take to North Platte when he moved Rocky up there. Roland and I were on our way by 7.15 in the morning. He screamed his distress at being separated from Rocky. A good loud horse neigh can carry two miles – which meant forty minutes of travel before Rocky was out of my earshot. Horses have better hearing than people and Roland carried on whinnying and looking behind for twenty minutes more. After that he generally kept a sad silence, although once or twice he hollered out to see if he could get a response from his friend. I felt bad about what I was doing to these two animals. Horses prefer the company of their own kind to that of people.

The Oregon Trail follows the south bank of the Platte river right through to Casper in Wyoming – about six hundred miles on from Kearny. The fort at Kearny had provided everything a garrison soldier could want – except for one thing and that was provided at a place four miles west of the fort. It was called Dirty Woman Ranch. I assume it was where the soldiers went with their dirty washing. Quite a town grew up around the ranch and it eventually became known as Central City. However, a much more respectable town started to grow on the other side of the river and Central City waned until the only business which remained was the Dirty Woman Ranch. It just goes to show that the best business investments are those in good traditional industries – like taking in laundry and such like.

My plan was to try to get to North Platte within four days, which would be by Thursday night. This was the week of the Nebraskaland Days which, as the posters said, 'are a whole week of rip roarin', knee slappin', toe tappin', hand clappin' fun for the whole family.' I had never been to a pukka rodeo and hoped to go. There were also a number of other fascinating items on the agenda, including a spitting competition and a hog calling event, as well as a shootout.

We would need to average just over twenty-five miles a day if I was to make the trip by Thursday night. I had no doubts about Roland, who was getting stronger and stronger by the day, although I had some reservations about my own reserves of stamina. We made remarkably good progress. It was really quite cool – no more than 80° F, and there was a good stiff breeze blowing. It was also much easier leading one horse than two. Rocky always wanted to walk faster than me whereas Roland's long slow pace suited me fine. But Rocky was still my favourite. He had a sparkle about him. He loved running and seemed to take a real pleasure in physical activity. He tackled everything with enthusiasm – especially his food. Rocky was an optimist. I even liked his ugliness.

Roland, on the other hand, was a dour plodder of a horse, a big beautiful dope. As I walked along I watched his feet eating up the miles. He walked straighter than any horse I had seen. Most horses, like people, wear their shoes down faster in one place than another. Some kick the toes out, others slide their feet on to the ground and wear away one side of the shoe. Roland could wear a set of shoes until they were as thin as tin foil. Each foot went down straight and true. Ask him to walk over some rough ground and he would likely fall flat on his face. He always had that wary look in his eye, as though he expected life to be bad to him.

Roland was a pessimist. I suspected that this trip was not contradicting his view of the world.

The Platte river lay quite close to a line running due west so I was able to find a county road which took us parallel to it. We spent the whole day no more than a mile from the track of the old Oregon Trail itself. At lunchtime I found a side road which went right to the banks of the river. Roland got a good bellyful of grass while I sat and watched the river slipping slowly past. It looked beautifully clear and I would have gone for a paddle except it would have meant removing and replacing all my plasters. I could not square this lovely clean river with the emigrant description of the Platte as being a dirty silty apology for a river. I looked at the map again and noticed a number of flood control schemes and reservoirs to the west. The Platte river has been tamed and brought to heel by man. There are times, I thought, when man's interference does manage to improve things.

By 4.30 in the afternoon we had made twenty-five miles and I was beginning to think that travelling with one horse was better than travelling with two. I started looking out for somewhere suitable to stay. I was beginning to get the hang of sizing up likely places. Farms were best, especially those with a large grass-covered yard or a pasture close to the house. I could tether Roland for the night but I would sleep better if I knew that he was safely in a field. All I really needed was grass, a tap and a place to pitch the tent.

A big white Cadillac stopped and a lady asked me where I was headed. I spent a few minutes telling her about my journey. When I asked if she knew anywhere that I could stay, she said that I could stop at her husband's farm. She gave me directions and drove off. I looked at the map and saw that her farm was a full seven miles further on down the road. Thirty-two miles is a long way to walk in a day.

Roland had a large field to himself and Mrs Carson invited me to supper. It was a big one. Afterwards I did not sleep well because there was a fearful thunderstorm and I had pitched my tent under some trees. I was not all that worried about lightning but I could see several fallen branches lying in the grass around the tent. Some were larger than I would have liked.

When I got up the next morning my feet were killing me. It was not so much the blisters as a really painful ache in the heels. Blisters are damage that you can see, this was something new. I walked up and down the road to see if the pain would ease. It did. So I packed up and carried on west.

The river and the trail started to swing away north-west. The south side of the river was extremely rural: lots of farms with dirt section roads. It would be ideal travelling except that again all the roads went north/south or east/west. They refused to go in the right direction. The north side of the river had the railway, Interstate 80 freeway and the much older Highway 30 running along within two miles of its banks. In British terms Interstate 80 was a motorway and the other an A road. Both followed the curve of the Platte river and headed straight for the town of North Platte. I had a simple choice – stay on the south side of the river on the quiet back roads but take an extra day to get to North Platte, or cross the river at Lexington and travel along Highway 30 to save myself twenty miles. I made a bad mistake when I decided to take the short route.

We crossed the river – not without some games from Roland – and called into McDonald's at Lexington. I took Roland in through the drive-in section. We stopped at the board where you are supposed to shout your order. I said 'Hello'. There was no reply. I shouted again. No reply. The traffic started to build up behind us. A large jowled lady in the car behind sounded her horn. She wanted her hamburger and Roland and I were standing between her and instant gratification. I shouted again. Then the man from three cars back got out and came up to me to explain that the sign had a metal detector on it to tell the people in McDonald's when someone was waiting for service. Roland and I were not metallic enough to trip it off. He then explained this to the fat lady and got her to drive forwards.

Then a voice from the box said, 'Hi there, can I help you?' Roland swung around and narrowly missed the impatient lady's car. She gave us a jowly scowl. I am not sure that she liked Englishmen.

I placed my order and went around to the window where you pay for the food before collecting it. The girl at the window turned her face in my direction and delivered her well-trained smile as she took my money. She then looked back at her till. Roland was peering over my right shoulder at her. She handed me the change, smiled at us again and wished us a nice day as she returned her attention to the till. It was proof positive that service with a smile was the result of staff training rather than true job satisfaction. I walked along to the next window to collect my order. The girl at the window spotted Roland immediately and gave out a great hoot. She must have been new to the job and had not yet been turned into a polite automaton.

I ate my Big Mac, two large fries, apple pie, cherry pie, large Coke and coffee on the grass beside the car park. I was after all walking over twenty-five miles a day. One of the girls came out to ask me what I was doing and where I was going. She had been sent by the restaurant manager 'because there were twenty curious staff in there whose minds were only half on the job'. Maybe they were human after all.

I turned west on Highway 30 to find that it was much busier than I had thought. Worst of all it had just one lane in either direction and no hard shoulder. We were forced to walk in the main stream of traffic. Most of the cars or trucks swung well clear of us over to the other side of the road – provided there was no traffic coming the other way. If there was an oncoming vehicle then they had no choice but to come in close to Roland and me. They could have slowed right down, I suppose, and waited for the road to clear, but that option was not one that appealed to many people. After a couple of near-misses I decided that I had to get off the road whenever I thought that two vehicles would cross close to us. I walked along keeping an eye on the traffic in both directions. When I saw cars coming both ways I walked Roland into the scrub at the side of the road and waited for them to pass. If that was not bad enough, the railway line ran along fifty yards from the road. Every twenty minutes or so a massive coal train would come rumbling along the American Pacific railway line. It was perfectly horrible – and dangerous as well.

After ten miles of this purgatory both Roland and I were wound up as tight as coil springs. We faced another fifty stressful miles before getting to North Platte.

I found a place to stay for the night, saw to Roland's needs and climbed into the tent to hide from the world. I lay there listening to the cars swishing past on Highway 30. Their presence was fleeting and repetitive – like a cartoon sketch. The trains were a different matter. They stayed in earshot for fifteen minutes or more. They were like a full, deep, dark oil-painting of sound. I could hear them hooting and wailing as they passed through Lexington ten miles to the east. Then there were a few minutes silence before a subliminal rumble would grow into a hum. It would rise, gaining colour and depth until it became the sound of a train. The leviathan came ever closer and closer until it was pounding past within fifty feet of where I was lying in my tent with my back pressed firm against the ground. I could feel the earth heaving and straining under the sudden 1,000-ton burden.

I had never camped this close to the railway before. The trains made a complete spectrum of noises, from the high-pitched squeal of sick bearings to the stentorian rumble of wheels on expansion joints. But the sounds went even deeper, right through to a vibration so deep that it could only be experienced as it came up through my back lying on the Nebraskan turf. The mile-long trains travel slowly – they take three minutes to pass a single spot. A three-minute-long crescendo of noise and vibration.

I lit my candle and looked at the map to count the miles from where I lay to North Platte. However I counted, it was always well over fifty. I noticed that I had camped close to a place called Midway Station. It was one of the many trading posts which opened up along the trail during the 1850s and 1860s. These posts were the early forerunners of the motorway services and often had a blacksmith's shop and a store where flour, bacon and coffee could be bought – all at hugely inflated prices. The station owners made a lot of money by trading in livestock. They would buy exhausted oxen or mules from the emigrants at knock-down prices, then rest them and feed them up to sell to the next train through, again at the sort of mark-up which makes modern car-dealers seem philanthropic.

As the trail developed and became a regular stage run, the emigrants might expect to find a supply station every twenty or thirty miles. To have called this one Midway Station suggests a cruel marketing ploy. The emigrants might assume that it was halfway to Oregon and therefore a good place to celebrate and spend more money than they would otherwise have.

I fell asleep listening to the BBC World Service. Four Englishmen were trying to talk on the subject of beer glasses for one minute without hesitation, repetition or deviation.

The next morning I tried walking on the wrong side of the road, facing the oncoming traffic. It was no better, and had the disadvantage of confusing the drivers. The constant aggravation of dealing with the traffic whizzing past us at fifty-five miles an hour was slowly ratchetting up the stress on both Roland and me. We were losing our ability to deal with the traffic.

I think that the morning of 19 June was the low spot of
the trip – and possibly my life up to that point. The circumstances of my situation rattled and bumped around and
around inside my head. I had made too many mistakes. The
first was in trying to do the trip by myself and against a
deadline. I mentally ticked off my other misfortunes and
failures: I had one horse off sick because of my own incom-
petence; my feet were killing me; I was running the risk of
killing myself, Roland and possibly several innocent American motorists; I was so far behind schedule that I did not
think that I would even make it to Oregon; I was missing
my family and the last letter I had managed to get from my
wife had the glad tidings that she had been forced to put
down my dog. And why was I doing this to myself and
these unfortunate American horses which would have been
much happier had I never entered their lives? That was the
hardest question of all.

To cap it all I knew that I was incredibly lucky to have
the opportunity to get myself into this situation – to fulfil
the dream of riding the Oregon Trail. How ungrateful can a
person get?

When you are feeling down it is hard to remember that
the world can be a great place – and for me it was about to
change for the better. It was all thanks to the driver of a
yellow van. I do not know why but I noticed it as it went
past me for the first time. Then it came back the other way.
It was a full twenty minutes before it came past again. It
pulled up in a layby in front of me and a man with
wire-rimmed spectacles, a full beard and long hair got out.
He waved at me. I knew that I had seen his face before: I
recognised him from the pictures Oscar Krause had shown
me back at Westmoreland, Kansas. It was the man who had
organised the pack train of mustangs from St Louis to
Jackson Hole in Wyoming.

'Jim Brookover,' I said as I approached. We shook hands.
'Oscar told me to keep an eye out for you,' said Jim. 'I

know just what you are going through right now, buddy. You are feeling that you must be mad to do this and that you want to pack up right now.'

Jim took Roland's lead rope from my hand and took us over to the side door of his van. He produced a bucketful of water for Roland and handed me a big paper bag from a local take-away. It contained chicken, mashed potato, cole-slaw and a large container of iced tea. It was absolutely perfect. I have never tasted food so good. I even enjoyed the iced tea.

Jim Brookover was one of the few people in America who knew what I was feeling like just then. He had done over ten thousand miles of long-distance horse riding. He knew that there would be bad moments in doing a trip like this. He could see from my face that I was having one.

He said that he had some really good news for me. He pointed over towards the Union Pacific railway line which was about fifty feet away from where we were standing at the side of the road. He told me that every railway track in the USA has a service road running alongside it. Technically it is private property but Jim said that the signs telling the public to keep off were there just to keep the lawyers happy. Without them, the railroad company would be responsible for every idiot who decided to commit suicide by throwing themselves under a train.

I walked across to the railway line. Sure enough, a well-maintained dirt road ran right alongside. I had been struggling with the cars and trucks of Highway 30 for a day and a half while a perfect, traffic-free track lay no more than fifty feet away.

'I see that you are limping pretty bad,' said Jim as I walked back towards him. He told me that he could find me a place to stay in a town called Brady.

'But it is twenty-three more miles up the road, do you think you can walk that far?' he asked. I thought that I could but Jim suggested that he take my gear in his van, which would allow me to ride the horse. 'Unless you would regard that as cheating,' he said.

I had to think about that for a while. I suppose that I had started cheating when I decided to let Park Trooper Joe take Rocky to North Platte in his horse-trailer. I had been walking a lot of the time so I was no longer making the trip under horsepower alone. I decided that allowing Jim to take my equipment would be no worse than sending Rocky ahead by trailer.

I felt pretty good that afternoon as I rode Roland down the Union Pacific maintenance road. In the space of half an hour my entire outlook had changed. I was back riding after well over a hundred miles of walking, I had a bellyful of food, an offer of a bed for the night and a field for Roland. I had also met someone who understood my predicament and who could offer me good practical advice. Jim had persuaded me that getting as far as North Platte was quite an achievement and I was back to feeling optimistic about my prospects.

11

Buffalo Bill, dental bill and killer horses

Brady to North Platte is a mere twenty miles and I was confident that we would arrive at the Buffalo Bill Ranch by mid-afternoon. There were times when the railroad and its maintenance road swung out and away from Highway 30. Then the journey became more like a stroll through the countryside – save for the occasional train thundering past. It felt marvellous to be on the road and travelling. I could not believe that twenty-four hours earlier I had been so close to giving up. I began to notice the ant nests, which could be found every ten or fifteen yards along the track. They appeared as three-foot discs of bare soil which shimmered with activity as the ants bustled around in confused circles. Roland and I must have killed hundreds of thousands of ants as we came tromping through their front yards. It is hard to imagine what they found to live off – apart from the rubbish thrown from the trains. And there was plenty of that. The maintenance road was strewn with small white plastic bottles and sweet wrappers. Union Pacific train drivers must have rotten teeth and huge dental bills.

The trains came along every half hour or so. At first I walked Roland out into the grass verge so that he could face them as they came through but he soon got used to these rumbling monsters which came thundering towards us – only to miss us by four or five feet. There was always a bored-looking driver sitting in the front engine of the four units, while the cab of the third always seemed to contain a man who sat reading a newspaper. I thought that he could be a spare driver having a rest, although the job of a modern engine driver did not seem to be particularly arduous. I wondered whether the man who read the paper got much satisfaction from his job. Earlier in my trip I had seen a train stopped at a drive-in burger bar while a man carried a tray laden with fast food out to his mates in the train. It would be enough to have the hard men of our own Great Western pinwheeling in their graves.

Roland and I walked gingerly around a snake which had its head wedged in a tin can. It was writhing and flailing around in the sand. I stopped for a moment and wondered about trying to help it get out of its predicament. I remembered my feelings of guilt about that mother possum I had seen lying in the road in Kansas. I did not know whether the snake was poisonous or not but Roland was extremely wary of it so I decided to let him be my guide. We walked on, leaving the snake in its suffering.

As we approached the town of North Platte the railway rejoined the road. We passed an airfield and I noticed a pedestrian walking along the side of Highway 30. He was smartly dressed with a nice white shirt and a sober tie, and he was carrying his jacket slung over his shoulder. He was making no attempt to thumb a lift. I had seen plenty of pedestrians in the towns we had passed through but people walking in the countryside are a rare commodity in the mid-west. This man was only the sixth in over six hundred miles of travelling through the prairies. I walked over and asked him if he had time to take some pictures of Roland and me. He seemed very happy to oblige and told me that he was only killing time. A man must have plenty of it to spare if he squanders it by taking walks along the side of Highway 30.

'You should know,' said John Ehrig with a smile.

It turned out that he was a charter pilot who had just brought a group of businessmen to North Platte from Omaha on the other side of Nebraska. He was due to take them back that evening. His job as a flying bus driver meant that he had to spend a lot of time hanging around airports. It seemed strange that it had taken him just over an hour to fly the same distance I had travelled in six weeks.

John Ehrig became a pilot after leaving school. Then he decided to fulfil his real ambition, which was to become an engine driver. His ambition fulfilled, and his bank manager barking at his heels, John Ehrig went back to being a pilot again. I asked him about the man who reads the paper in the cab of the third engine. John told me that he was the brake-man. It had once been his job to make sure that the train was still attached to the engine – pretty important when you are in a train over a mile long. He used to ride in the caboose and apply the brakes when going downhill – but that went out with the introduction of fail-safe pressure brake systems. They kept him on in his caboose so that if one of the couplings on the train broke he could run back up the line to warn any following trains. His purpose has been taken away by the technology contained in a hundred-dollar black box which is fixed to the last truck but the job has been preserved by the unions. It sounded like a story from Britain in the 1970s not America in the 1990s.

John Ehrig told me that the Buffalo Bill Ranch was right on the other side of North Platte. He suggested that I take a route through the northern outskirts of town. My twenty-mile day suddenly turned into a twenty-five-mile day.

Roland and I entered the town through an industrial area of warehouses, lorry parks and factories. Suddenly, Roland started to sing out with his high-pitched whinny. Again and again he sent his ululating calls out across the warehouses and homes of North Platte. I could not make out what was up. Then I started to hear answering calls from other horses coming back to us. The frantic messaging to and fro con-tinued until I saw a large area of stockyards along one side of the road. Several of them were full of horses.

It was the North Platte killer horse plant – one of the largest in the United States. It is here that old horses are turned into dog food. Younger ones are cut up into frozen packs of meat and sent to France for human consumption.

Any slaughterhouse is a pathetic place. The transition between warm breathing animal and cold, shrink-wrapped slab of meat is enough to make any human being feel uncomfortable. I cannot put my fork into a piece of meat without the sights, smells and sounds of the slaughterhouse coming to mind. These places represent the ultimate in human exploitation of another species.

Small animals like sheep and pigs are herded, five or six at a time, into stunning pens. There they meet a man who is armed with a pair of giant tongs which he places on either side of the animal's head. A huge jolt of electricity stuns the pig or sheep into insensibility. The back legs are then hooked to a chain and the animal is hoisted up on to an overhead railway. The throat is then cut to allow the life-blood to come gushing out into a wide gutter. An efficiently run slaughterhouse will be dealing with one pig or sheep every seven seconds.

Big animals like cattle or horses are forced, one at a time, to walk into a narrow box. A gate is slammed shut behind them and a man leans down towards their head. He is looking for a particular spot in the middle of the forehead. He draws two imaginary lines, one from right ear to left eye, the other from left ear to right eye. He places the business end of a humane killer where the lines cross. There is a bang as a short rod of metal shoots out and enters the brain of the horse or the cow. The steel rod retreats to its hiding place inside the humane killer to await its next victim.

A lever is pulled and the floor of the pen drops away to allow the animal to fall, kicking and thrashing, to a lower level. It is already dead. The kicking is just the nervous system firing off impulses at random. So I am told. Another man comes forward. He is armed with a two-foot length of stainless steel spring. He shoves it in through the hole in the middle of the animal's forehead and waggles it around. This creates even more frantic thrashing from the cow or horse.

The spring is to mash the nervous system so that it will not kick or move as its legs are chained to the overhead railway. The death throes of a half-ton cow or horse can kill an unwary or unlucky slaughterman.

The animal is lifted up and away through to a room where its throat is cut, the skin is peeled back, the hooves and tail are removed and the head is cut off. Then a large power-saw is used to cut the skinned carcass into two halves and it no longer looks like an animal.

I remember being taken around the back of a slaughter-house to be shown the place where the hides and intestines and other valueless bits come sliding down bloody ramps to land in huge skips. The warm piles of animal remains steamed on the chilly November day. The skip of skinned cattle heads was the worst of all. The muscles still twitched, the eyes continued to move in their sockets.

Cattle and sheep go meekly to their ends. Pigs are more intelligent. They seem to know what is happening and they scream warnings to those that follow behind.

I have never been to a horse slaughterhouse but I have been to one where worn-out dairy cattle are turned into hamburgers, beef sausages and cheap pies. These animals had lived in close association with people for a decade or more. Twice a day they had gone into a milking parlour where a man had offered them food in return for their milk. They knew men and their ways and allowed themselves to be exploited. They trusted people – and I thought I could see betrayal on their faces as they received the death blow.

The horses in the yards at North Platte could not have known what was coming to them – but I did. This was the place where cow ponies, draught horses and family pets ended their days. These animals had spent their lives in the service of man. A one-way trip to the North Platte horse slaughterhouse was their reward.

Roland was still hollering to his new friends at the slaughterhouse as we came into the residential parts of town. Mid-western towns are terribly alien to English eyes. North Platte has a population of 23,000 but the people and houses are splattered over a huge area. An English town of the same area would contain five times as many people. But land in the mid-west is cheap; town houses are well spread out – even the rotten ones. In Britain, where land is expensive, such houses would have been repaired and renovated. In America they can pass down through the social strata, their gardens accumulating more junk and old cars as the quality of the neighbourhood falls. British houses with such large grounds would have well-kept gardens but then we have a good climate for gardening: it is seldom too hot or too cold for working outside and we do not have to irrigate our flower-beds and lawns.

While British towns have grown in an organic, haphazard way over hundreds, sometimes thousands, of years, American towns have been planned. Their roads follow the compass, not some archaic and long-gone field system. Sudden unexpected bends in British high streets can be traced back to a boggy patch in a twelfth-century farm lane. American high streets run straight and true, throwing side-streets off to right and left, and demonstrating a surveyor's enthusiasm for right angles and good order.

The sense of good order extends even to the naming of the streets. North Platte has 1st, 2nd and 3rd Street, continuing all the way up to 23rd Street. It has A to M Streets. It has roads named after trees – Elm, Poplar, Cottonwood, Sycamore, Ash and Maple. It has presidents: Wilson and Roosevelt. Then there are the generals: Custer, Sherman and Jackson. But the accountants, surveyors and nit-pickers did not have it all their own way. There is an Easy Street, and for that I am grateful.

Rocky, Roland and Dylan. Right at the beginning I had no more of an idea about what lay ahead of us than the horses. Ignorance can be a dangerous travelling companion.

Far too much stuff - and at the time I thought that I had cut my possessions to the bare minimum.

The horses started out being very fussy about water - by the end of the second week they would drink anything I put in front of them.

Water in the desert. Without water - 40 acres per cow. With water - one cow per acre. It was wonderfully cool along the roads beside the irrigated fields.

Prairie trains: long, slow, noisy. I became a compulsive wagon counter, hoping for the perfect 100.

At 20 miles a day it takes an awfully long time to get across the Great Plains - which are now the world's bread basket.

The mules. So much stamina, power and cussedness in an ugly package - at least that's what I thought at the beginning.

The local police usually turned out to help the wagon train through built-up areas.

Jesse's mules always took the lead on the river crossings - with their driver cussing all the way. Once we

...velling with the wagon train I felt that there were people always on hand to help with the difficult sections.

A mixed team of a mustang and mule - and the mustang was boss.

I came to realise that I should have bought mules rather than horses.

Life on the road with the wagon train - all my gear is in one of the support trucks.

The Great Plains are not always flat, there are places where they roll like ocean waves made solid.

The wagon trainers settle down to watch a video - about wagon trains.

Rocky and his new family - he became the perfect family horse, well mannered and athletic.

People watched us as we walked through their neighbourhood. A few kids asked if they could stroke the horse – which Roland enjoyed greatly. A Mexican migrant worker offered him a cabbage – which he enjoyed even more. I tried to make conversation while Roland munched but the man spoke hardly a word of English. I had fewer reasons than he for feeling homesick.

We arrived at the Buffalo Bill Ranch around four in the afternoon. It is on the western side of town, right beside the rodeo grounds. North Platte is the place where Buffalo Bill came to die – his house is now a state park.

The Buffalo Bill Ranch also has a dude ranch where the visitors can rent horses for a one-hour trail ride. Roland let out one of his ear-piercing whinnies when he saw the other horses and was rewarded with a barrage of sound coming back at us. He suddenly got very excited, lifted his head and warbled out another call. Just one horse responded this time. The two of them sang back and forth as we came down the road. Roland clearly knew where Rocky was long before I did. He had managed to pick Rocky's voice out from the noise of the other horses.

As we came closer to the ranch, the loud whinnies from my two horses softened to that whickering noise which emanates from somewhere deep in the back of their throats. I had a lump in mine as the two of them touched nuzzles over the fence. I unloaded Roland's pack, threw it down on the ground and went over to introduce myself to the girls who run the dude ranch on behalf of the State of Nebraska.

I asked where I should pitch my tent and the girls told me that I could use the camp-bed in the superintendent's office. There I had the use of a big sink with running hot water, a toilet and air-conditioning. There was also a large collection of books about Buffalo Bill Cody. The thought of spending an evening in that air-conditioned office and reading a book or two was just wonderful to contemplate. I settled myself in, got cleaned up and then went out to explore the rest of the facilities at the Buffalo Bill Ranch.

It is now a tourist attraction where visitors can see the house where the great man lived out his last few years. There is also a massive and elaborate barn where Buffalo Bill Cody kept the stock and equipment for the Wild West Show which he took on tour all around America and Europe. In the next couple of hours and in the superintendent's office later that evening I learned a fair bit about Buffalo Bill. I also got to see Americans on vacation in their own country. When they come to England they wear over-bright shirts, shorts which are too long or slacks which are too short and trainers which are too big. I assumed that they only said 'gee honey' to each other because they knew it amused us English. It had never occurred to me that they try to be terribly discreet when they come to Britain. In its natural environment the American tourist feels free to 'gee honey' its mate as loudly and as often as it likes, to wear real headache-makers of shirts and even more bizarre sartorial concoctions on its lower half. I loved them. I only had to open my mouth to make a comment to the person beside me and I had a friend for life. In the space of an hour I was invited by half a dozen groups to join them at supper either at the local pizza parlour or back at their trailer. There is not a nation in the world to beat the Americans at their hospitable best.

Buffalo Bill actually turned out to be a bit of a disappointment. He was a Pony Express rider for a short time. He was then a wholly unexceptionable army scout who seemed to derive a great deal of pleasure from slaughtering huge numbers of buffalo. When he started his career there were plenty of these dopey, lumbering beasts to kill. At first he killed them for the sheer hell of it, later he killed them under contract to provide cheap meat for the navvies building the Union Pacific railway. Later on still, it became official government policy to eradicate the buffalo. The idea was that if you got rid of them, then you also got rid of the

Indians – who were starting to cause problems for the waves of white settlers coming across the continent. The plan worked really well. Suddenly Buffalo Bill found that the government was encouraging him in his hobby. He claimed to have shot over 4,200 buffalo in one season. A man was doing his patriotic duty by killing a buffalo, and Bill Cody was a patriotic man.

He undoubtedly starved more Indians to death by depriving them of their main source of food than he ever dispatched in combat. The whole lifestyle and economy of the Indian was linked to the huge herds of buffalo which they followed around the plains the way the Lapps follow their herds of caribou. Buffalo hides were used to make tepees, clothes, blankets and saddles. The meat was eaten fresh, although it could be dried to make tough but highly nutritious bits of yuck. Indian camps were surrounded by trellises which were festooned with buzzing colonies of flies. Under the flies were strips of buffalo meat which were slowly turning black under the sun and a crusty patina of fly droppings. The Indians and their dogs lived off the dried meat for a large part of the year. The appeal of dried buffalo meat might pall slightly during the winter – so when they wanted fresh meat they would eat the dogs. Westerners who stayed in Indian camps and who lived off Indian food said that the high protein diet played hell with their digestion and turned their urine deep dark stinking yellow.

Under a combination of starvation and physical threats, the Indian chiefs signed treaties confining them to certain tracts of land and allowing the white man dominance over other parts. The Indians got the scabby bits, the whites got the best. In any case the Indians were nomadic and found the concept of land ownership difficult to grasp. It was like signing away rights to air or to light.

Eventually the Indians realised that they had been sold a dummy. Without the buffalo their whole economy collapsed. Immigrant population pressure continued to rise.

White incursions of Indian land increased. Treaties were ignored. It was a pathetic and humiliating end.

Buffalo Bill found that he no longer had a real job, so he went into show business. He took his cowboys and Indians back east and showed the townies what the wild west was never really like. He staged Indian raids on stage coaches, re-created famous robberies and thrilled the public with trick riding of all sorts.

The show was a success and Cody was well on his way to becoming rich. Then a series of Indian uprisings occurred, culminating in the defeat and death of General Custer at Little Big Horn. Cody saw his opportunity to become disgustingly rich. He made a highly publicised return to army scouting. He claimed to have 'taken the first scalp' in revenge for the death of his 'friend' General George Armstrong Custer. This single statement demonstrates two terrible flaws in Bill Cody's character. The first was that he was prepared to indulge in the uncivilised business of taking scalps. The second was that he was proud of being a friend of General Custer.

Custer was to military strategy what Nixon is to integrity. He came thirty-fourth out of a class of thirty-four at his military academy. He suffered from a fatal combination of ignorance and a lust for glory which prompted him to lead his men into certain and completely unnecessary annihilation at the battle of Little Big Horn – which became known as Custer's Last Stand.

Once Buffalo Bill Cody had finished milking every conceivable ounce of publicity out of his return to scouting he left his army colleagues to get on with emasculating the Indian nation and returned to showmanship. Custer's Last Stand became an essential part of the Buffalo Bill Wild West Extravaganza, which was even bigger and better than it ever was before. It pulled in huge audiences. This inglorious chapter of American history was dressed up as a heroic defeat. A small band of men, representing civilisation and all things good, were overcome by a numerically superior, though morally inferior, force of barbarians. Cody's Wild West Show was the sort of theatrical spectacle which had not been seen since the Roman circus and would not appear until Cecil B. DeMille came along thirty years later.

Buffalo Bill built a twenty-room mansion and the fanciest barn in the country on the outskirts of North Platte and settled down to die. His home is now owned by the State of Nebraska and is a historic park. The 'gee honeys' stroll around in their shirts and sunglasses peering at the relics of the great man. They can see a flickering black and white film of the Wild West Show as it really was. The house, or 'mansion', has been redecorated the way Bill Cody had it done – flock wallpaper and over-stuffed sofas. The place says a lot about the way the image of the west has been marketed over the years.

I was just leaving when I noticed a pile of 'lucky' horse-shoes by the door – only a dollar each. They did not look right somehow. A few were worn down the way you would expect an old shoe to be but most were almost new and some were 'correction' shoes which had been specially made to fit horses with bad feet.

As I looked through the pile one of the ladies on duty asked me if I would like to buy one. I asked her where they came from. She looked slightly uncomfortable. She grinned, she shrugged, she blushed.

'Go on, you can tell me. I promise I won't tell anyone else.' At the time I thought that I was telling the truth. I now see that I told a lie.

'They come from the killer horse plant on the other side of town,' she said, using the traditional American euphem-ism for slaughterhouse. Calling cull horses killer horses makes it sound as though it is they who do the killing.

The pile of shoes reminded me of the heaps of false teeth you see in those doom-laden black and white photographs taken at Belsen or Auschwitz. I wondered how many people would have paid their dollar if they knew that the shoes had been ripped from the feet of freshly killed horses. For his part, I think that Buffalo Bill might have been quite pleased to think that his front room was still being used to market the west to an unsuspecting public.

12

Bull-dogging, chilli dogs, a bovine dominator and an English coward

The law says that every rodeo must have a vet in atten-
dance, so I arranged to meet the local horse doctor at the
Nebraskaland rodeo grounds that evening. Gerry Woolford
said that he would be happy to give the horses the once
over and to give me his opinion on Rocky's feet.

As I rode Rocky with Roland in tow towards the
stadium grounds I could hear the commentator opening the
proceedings. As soon as he heard the tannoy, Rocky started
to prance and get excited. He obviously was remembering
his years as a rodeo horse and was expecting to be allowed
to join in. I felt like I was sitting on an unexploded bomb.
Rocky had been used in calf-roping competitions and also
for bull-dogging. The latter is an event where a cowboy
gallops alongside a steer, jumps out of the saddle, grabs the
steer by the horns and then wrestles the surprised creature
to the ground.

I was a bit early for the appointment with the vet, so I
watched the opening ceremony from the jiggling platform
of Rocky's back. I had a good view but Rocky was less than
calm. His eyes popped with excitement, his ears were
pricked forwards and his nostrils flared as his keen senses
soaked up the familiar sights, sounds and smells. Rocky had
been here before and was getting all steamed up and ready
to go. Every now and again he would start cantering on the
spot – a most unsettling feeling for me sitting up on his

back. For his part, Roland had that worried look in his eye and merely pressed closer to his excited companion.

American rodeos follow a common pattern. They always seem to start with a women's horseback drill team who canter around the arena wearing white cowboy hats and cast-iron, one-hundred-percent flop-proof brassieres. These are worn under pink or puce satin shirts which shimmer in the floodlights. Western women seem to wear their years remarkably well. Most members of drill teams have pretty good figures no matter how old they are. But there always seems to be one team member who is carrying rather too much weight or, to be more accurate, whose horse is being forced to carry too much weight. She will flop and bounce her way through the routine as her mount struggles and strains under the burden. The gyrating flesh makes rider, horse and audience feel uncomfortable. The drill team at North Platte had a perfect example in their midst.

The commentary box was manned by two identical moustaches called Randy and Hadley – they shared the same deep mid-western voices and a sense of humour with the quirky unpredictability of a pre-war German railway timetable. One of the commentators introduced the drill team as 'The Cheyenne Frontier Days Dandies', who were, according to Randy, or it might have been Hadley, 'regular performers at the Buffalo Bill Rodeo here at North Platte and who always come on Friday and Saturday nights to let us enjoy their talents'. I am still not sure whether the *double entendres* were deliberate.

Randy handed the microphone over to Arlene Kensinger, the 'den mother' of the Cheyenne Dandies. She called out their names as her protégées came into the ring two by two, their banners and long hair streaming in the wind behind them. Their family names served as reminders of the northern Europeans who had settled the plains over a century ago – names such as Hayes, Myers, Wettner, Petch and Bailey. But their Christian names were all American – Brandy,

Mandy, Darlene, Tricia and Lachelle. They celebrated the newness of America as a nation.

The galloping and manoeuvring of the well-turned-out human and equine horse flesh, the figures of eights and the snake patterns, the fluttering flags and false eyelashes made a striking sight – which was almost completely ignored by the crowd. They were too busy finding seats and consuming junk food: popcorn in cartons the size of tea-chests, coke in cups big enough for an advertising agency rubber plant to call home and fistfuls of bizarre things called chilli dogs. These are glistening rods of meat, dipped in batter and deep-fried to fatty perfection – a brilliant way of persuading the American public to eat the sweepings from the floor of the slaughterhouse.

After ten minutes of almost precision drilling, the twelve sweaty horses and twelve sweaty maidens and matrons of the Cheyenne Dandies left the ring and Hadley/Randy reclaimed the microphone. The rodeo proper was about to start. Or perhaps not. Judging by the people waiting to take the ring this was also going to involve a lot of galloping around in circles with banners streaming.

At the front of the queue of riders was an attractive young woman in a spangly shirt and extraordinarily tight jeans. Sewn or sprayed on I would guess. As Hadley announced the 1991 Rodeo Queen, she straightened her back and contorted her crimson, sports-car-shiny lips into a Sue Ellen smile. She raised her right hand to shoulder height in an oath-swearing position and started to semaphore it from side to side. On the word from Randy at the microphone, she spurred her horse into action and galloped off into the ring. The glamorous job of being a rodeo queen is not all that easy. She has to smile and wave at the crowd at the same time as controlling an excited horse which is galloping around the ring at full tilt. This is achieved with the help of the 'rodeo queen smile' where the face is pointed at the crowd but the eyes are firmly glued to the front to see where the horse is heading. It gives the queen a rather shifty look but at least it allows her to monitor the direction of her horse.

Randy called the rest of the queue of banner-bearers into the ring. Most of them were women from the North Platte drill team, called 'The Velvet Spurs' – an interesting mix of sexually laden concepts. Their banners turned out to represent the events of the evening – one each for the bull riding, the barrel racing, the roping and so on. Then there were banners for the main sponsors: Dodge Trucks and Wrangler Jeans. Then the flag of 'The Great State of Nebraska' was fluttered into the ring.

Hadley took a deep breath. His voice changed gear and his whole manner and diction altered as the Stars and Stripes was brought into the Rodeo arena. Suddenly the bonhomie had gone. His voice seeped sincerity with every syllable, his lips dribbled deference as he immersed himself in a script with enough cloying sentimentality to stick in the throat of Hughie Green. Had Hadley not been a rodeo commentator he would have been a knock-out TV evangelist or actor in *Knotts Landing* – he made Billy Graham sound like a stand-up comic. Hadley, or possibly Randy, could turn sincerity on and off like a tap.

The script plumbed the deepest chasms of sentimental imagery. It spoke of the white stripes of liberty, the red stripes of courage, the field of blue of loyalty. Hadley mentioned how this great flag had flown in places less glamorous than this. I started thinking of the camp sites, swimming pools, car showrooms and truck stops which bristled with American flags but Hadley spoke of Iwo Jima, Korea, Vietnam and more recently the Persian Gulf.

'Ladies and gentlemen, the free-est nation in the world should sound out tonight and let the rest of the world know how it feels to be free. Say hello to your own flag, will you do that for me tonight.'

I looked around to see that everyone was on their feet,

hand on heart. Beside me a big man was sitting on a horse waiting to go into the arena. He held his hat in his hand and glared angrily at me. I smiled back. He glared some more. His hat hand twitched in the direction of my head. I realised that I was the only one at the rodeo grounds still wearing a hat. I snatched it from my head – and he smiled wildly at me. I felt completely forgiven for my sin. Wonderful people the western Americans. A member of the English county set would have gone on glaring at me.

Then Hadley called upon the local songstress, Deb Rosentrader, to sing the American national anthem. The song is both a blessing and curse on the American people. It is a beautiful piece of music which makes our own 'God Save the Queen' sound like a trite funeral dirge. When sung well by a trained and talented female voice as a solo, the American national anthem is a soaring tribute to America and its people. Unfortunately, the 'Star Spangled Banner' requires a formidable vocal range and the ability to hold notes for long periods at both ends of the scale. The British national anthem, on the other hand, is designed to be mumbled by drunks. Even the tone-deaf can make a pretty good stab at singing it.

Deb Rosentrader was better than most but still not good enough to escape garnering some wincing sympathy from the crowd, despite her spirited attack on the song. She was not helped by the bucking bronc which chose that precise moment to make an equally spirited attempt at escaping from the pens underneath the announcers' stand.

Preliminaries over, the rodeo started for real.

Rodeos began 150 years ago as competitions between local ranch hands. It was a team event when cowpokes showed each other how good they were. Roping and bronc riding were the only events. Then some idiot decided to show how brave he was by climbing up on to the back of a bull. For a while chariot racing was popular, so was chuck wagon racing – both have faded.

The first event of the evening was the calf-roping – an
event which is guaranteed to bore the socks off the uniniti-
ated, especially at a quality rodeo like the one at North
Platte. A calf runs out of a chute at one end of the arena
chased by two horsemen. One cowboy is there just to keep
the calf running straight while the other throws a rope over
its head. His horse then slides to a halt and stops the calf
with a jerk. The cowboy gets off, throws the confused and
bruised calf to the ground and ties a short length of rope
around its legs – all in under ten seconds.

It is quite fascinating the first time you see it, the
second is interesting, by the time it comes to the third or
fourth you have started noticing the colour of the horses
or wondering whether you ought to go and try one of
those chilli dog things. The problem is that the better the
rodeo the better the competitors – at this level hardly
anyone misses or makes a mistake. The crowd gets to
watch calf after calf being roped and trussed up with a
regularity and economy of action which would have satis-
fied Henry Ford. There may only be three seconds
between the best and the worst. It makes county cricket
seem like a competitive sport.

The roping events at a local small-town rodeo make a
much better spectator sport. There is at least the chance that
someone will miss and people actually do. They also fall off
their horses, lose their temper, let go of their ropes, have
their saddles slip off. Everyone in the crowd knows everyone in the arena. One cowboy might get a polite round of
applause for finishing his roping in twelve seconds. Another
might get a standing ovation for achieving the trick in one
and a half minutes because this is the first time in eight years
that he has actually managed to get a rope around the damn
thing's neck.

I turned the horses away towards the back of the commentary box where Gerry Woolford had told me to meet
him. It was right beside the main thoroughfare where the

bull and bronc riders were passing through to the chutes where the animals waited for their riders. I sat and watched the procession of young men and the occasional doting girl-friend pass through to the competitors' stand. I watched them kiss each other goodbye as the women went to sit in the stand and the men went to meet the bulls and broncs they were due to ride that evening. The goodbye kiss was made in the knowledge that it could be the last – unlikely but possible.

There is a distinctive western way of dressing. Everyone wears a hat – few worth less than a hundred dollars. Shirts are brightly coloured, often with buttons, collars and cuffs in contrasting shades. Plenty of people wear waistcoats. Jeans are 'western cut' – tight on the bottom and left long in the leg so that they look right when the wearer is sitting in the saddle or on the top rail of a fence. Heavily tooled leather belts and fancy buckles are *de rigueur* for the western beau. I have a friend who lives in a wheelchair who says that he is an expert on the way that people hold their trousers up – belts and braces are at eye-level for him. British people wear terribly boring belts. He would love America.

Some of the competitors wore brightly coloured leather chaps which made them waddle like old sailors as they flapped around their legs. A few carried sports bags with the usual Adidas or Head labels on them. Most of the cowboys nodded and smiled politely at me as they walked past. They looked curiously at my saddle and a few made comments about the difficulty of sitting on a postage stamp or asked me what I had done with my saddle horn. I had heard this comment so often that I was ready with the reply that it was an English roping saddle which I had used to rope one of our large English bulls. He had taken the horn clear away. Not much of a joke I know but they laughed – possibly as much at my accent as my attempt at humour.

One young man wearing tight jeans, a white cowboy hat and a shiny red bomber-jacket swaggered up to me with that heel-clonking gate adopted by cowboy villains in cheap westerns. He was chewing gum.

'Howdy,' he said.

'Good evening,' I said.

'Nice looking horses. Strange saddle though,' he said.

'I'm English,' I said.

'Never have guessed,' he said.

I slipped off Rocky's back. It is rude to stay sitting imperiously on your horse when someone on foot is talking to you. The man ran his hand expertly over Roland. The speed of his gum chewing rose and fell as he ruminated on the condition of my horses. Then he looked Rocky over and picked up his bad foot.

'This the one you are worried about?' he said. I suddenly realised that this was Gerry Woolford, the North Platte vet. Roll over James Herriot.

I shook hands with Gerry and apologised for not knowing who he was. I explained that in England vets wear ties and jackets and hardly ever chew gum.

'Like in *All Creatures Great and Small* you mean,' said Gerry. It turned out that he was a real fan. He said it was one of the funniest programmes on TV. Perhaps he is right.

While he prodded and poked his pocket knife into the cracks and fissures in Rocky's hooves I asked Gerry if he was likely to be busy that evening.

'Never as busy as the human doctor is,' he said, flashing an impressive set of bright white teeth at me. Gerry checked Rocky's other feet and then straightened up.

'Is he up to completing the trip?' I asked.

'Well, he has got soft feet but if you can keep the moisture sealed in, grease them up a bit, he should make it. But he needs a three-week rest to grow some more hoof. It is no good expecting a farrier to try to put more nails into those cracks. The shoes will never stay on.'

Gerry confirmed, as diplomatically as possible, that if I had taken the precaution of treating Rocky's feet with hoof oil early on, then we could have avoided all the problems. He said that Roland was 'one heck of a tough horse' and would be able to walk on clear to the coast – 'and some ways past'. I asked Gerry about the chances of selling Rocky and buying another horse.

He told me that would be easy enough to do but Rocky was only worth his meat price – about six hundred dollars – and that was where he would end up if I tried selling him in North Platte. Not the sort of news I wanted to hear.

Gerry gave me a badge to get into the area around the commentary box and behind the chutes, and invited me to come back to see the rest of the rodeo once I had returned the horses to their borrowed paddock.

As I walked back to the rodeo grounds my mind was buzzing with the implications of Gerry's advice. If I waited for Rocky to get better I could kiss goodbye to ever catching the wagon train. I could sell him and buy another horse but that would take at least a week and Rocky would almost certainly wind up in the meat plant. His 'lucky' shoes would finish up in the pile at the Buffalo Bill Ranch. The thought made me feel slightly sick. He deserved better than that. I would also have to find another seven hundred dollars for another horse – who might be no better than Rocky and would certainly be less fit.

I did a calculation. My current rate of progress, plus a three-week layover, would get me to the end of the trail about halfway through October. The mountains would be getting dangerously cold by then. The only way I would ever get to ride a horse into Oregon City at the end of the trail was to cheat. I had been beaten. A bunch of kids came past on bikes. They shouted abuse at me and I had the solution to my transport problem.

By the time I got back to the rodeo grounds, a large black and heavily chromed pick-up truck and stock trailer was being driven into the arena. The legend 'John Payne – The Bovine Dominator' was written in large silvered letters along the side of the trailer. An extremely thin man, dressed in cowboy black, jumped out of the cab. he could be none other than the curiously named 'Bovine Dominator'.

'You will see something special here, bud,' said the man beside me in the competitors' stand. We had only exchanged a few words as I was taking my seat but we were firm friends already – possibly for life judging by the firmness of his handshake.

Soon after the Bovine Dominator had stepped out on to the dirt of the rodeo arena a chestnut horse sprang out of the back door of the trailer. It galloped around the ring until a crack of the Dominator's whip brought it skidding to a dust-generating halt. The Dominator swung up into the saddle and proceeded to gallop around the ring cracking his whip with one hand while the other remained tucked firmly into his belt. Randy the commentator explained that John Payne used to work for the electricity company until fifty thousand volts used him as a short-cut to earth. It cost him the use of his right arm and his job. It was while lying in hospital that he had dreamed up this award-winning rodeo speciality act.

'Watch this, Englishman,' said my new friend, accentuating the words by driving the wind from my body with a powerful jab of his elbow. I think he may have been a Texan. As I was retrieving my chilli dog from the floor, three Rottweilers were unceremoniously pushed out of the side door of the stock trailer. They looked bemused for a second. Then the Dominator cracked his whip and the three dogs started to run around the ring barking and snarling in a variety of satisfyingly theatrical ways. Randy told us that they were 'black-mouthed cur-head dogs out of Florida'. They still looked like Rottweilers to me. There must have been a good explanation as to why they had red handkerchiefs around their necks. I hoped that Hadley or Randy would tell us – but they decided that it was one piece of information the audience did not need to know.

The Dominator's sense of theatrical timing was perfect. I was just beginning to get bored with watching the dogs running and snarling when four long-horn steers emerged from the back of the trailer. The steers were large, rangy beasts with five-foot horn spans. The three dogs and John Payne with his bull whip gave chase. We were then treated to five minutes of frenzied cracking, whooping, snarling, barking and the generation of copious quantities of dust. The steers were persuaded, one at a time, to jump into the back of the pick-up and then along a ramp up on to the roof of the stock trailer. Once the bovines had been thoroughly dominated, John Payne rode his horse up on to the trailer, stood up on the saddle and cracked his whip over his head. The crowd thought it was fantastic and erupted with applause and cheering. I find it difficult to say why but his act, and the crowd's reaction to it, made me feel like a complete alien.

Then came one of the three most dangerous events of the evening, the bareback bronc riding. Bucking horses and bulls are not animals which have been brought fresh and wild off the range. They make their careers out of the job. They are bred for it. Their fathers and great-grandfathers may have been bucking and stomping on cowboys before finishing their careers at the meat plant. In many cases the bulls and horses are as well known as the cowboys who ride them. My new friend told me that 'real good cowboys, like my son' will take videos of the animals at work so that they know how they will behave once let out of the chute. The ropers will know each and every steer and calf brought to the rodeo by the stock contractor. Valuable form-sheets on the performance of individual animals are kept and can often change hands for hundreds of dollars.

The idea is not merely to stay on the wildly gyrating animal for the full eight seconds but also to spur vigorously every time it bucks. There is a huge amount of luck involved because points are awarded for each ride – half come from the performance of the horse and half from the man. If the cowboy is unlucky enough to draw a duff horse then he stands no chance of winning. Dave told me that there is a rodeo stock contractor who is sweating on whether or not his animals do well. If they do not perform then he will not be getting the job next year.

The horses which are used have a 'natural talent' for bucking which is enhanced by the fact that a sheepskin-covered strap is fitted around their belly, just in front of the back legs. The broncs also resent the presence of the cowboy, who is trying to gain as many points as possible by jabbing the horse with his spurs at every conceivable opportunity.

The cowboys get on to the horses in the chutes under the commentary box. They are not really chutes at all but narrow pens which hold the animals side-on to the arena. The gate is swung back and the horses leap out and into the ring. The bareback rider is allowed to hold on to a leather strap which goes around the horse where a saddle girth would be positioned. He tucks one hand tightly under this and hangs on. The other is used to 'grab sky' in a way guaranteed to catch the judge's eye. The hand and forearm must take a tremendous strain as the whole weight of the cowboy's body is jerked back and forth. At every buck the horse throws up his back legs so high that his rump bashes the cowboy in the back. The bareback cowboy has no control over the horse at all – some horses circle, others buck their way madly towards the edge of the arena only to turn away at the last moment.

When the eight seconds is up a hooter sounds and the pick-up men move in. One rides alongside the cowboy, who lets go with his hand and throws both arms around the waist of his rescuer. The other pick-up man then moves into the bucking horse to flip the buckle on the bucking strap. Only then does the bronc stop kicking and start looking for the way out of the ring.

Dave seemed happy to answer my questions about rodeo. His son was the third generation to have become involved in the sport. He told me that the bucking strap does not hurt the horse, it is merely an irritation which he wants to get rid of. I asked him if he thought it was cruel. He said that if he was a horse he would rather do the eight seconds a week than the eight hours a day I was getting my horses to do.

'So who is being cruel to horses then, limey?' He gave me a gappy smile.

I asked him why so many young men risk their lives in rodeo.

'Go over there and ask,' he said, waving in the direction of the area behind the chutes. 'They will tell you.'

A laconic cowboy with a badge saying 'security' waved me through to 'the chutes' once I had explained where I was from. It was an extraordinary place.

I remember as a child being taken below decks on an old naval ship with its wooden floors and low wooden ceilings. The sense of claustrophobia between the gun decks was heightened by the space of the outside world seen through the open gun-ports. And there was also a sense of danger; the suppressed fear, the aura created by the adrenalin of hundreds of scared men, had soaked into the timbers. There was a fearful energy to it.

The area behind the chutes at North Platte rodeo grounds had that same feeling – except it was real and alive. On one side of this narrow wooden tube was the arena with its baying crowd, on the other side were the pens where the bucking horses and massive bulls waited their turn to take on the cowboys. There must have been fifty men there. Young men in their late teens or early twenties. Boyish faces and boyish figures.

As each was called he would move to the chute, climb over the top and lower himself on to the horse's back. He would take a firm grip of girth with his gloved right hand. The kicking strap was placed around the back end of the horse. When the signal was given the strap was sweated up and the cowboy was given a good luck pat on the back as the chute gate was thrown back. The broncs are trained to lurch out into the ring, leaping high and to one side as they go. As the previous rider came back to the chutes he was commiserated with or congratulated on his performance.

The cowboys were competing against each other. Prizes are awarded only for the first three places, the rest would lose their hundred-dollar entrance fee. I had expected an atmosphere of competition rather than co-operation but these men were helping and consoling each other. There were bonds being formed here which would last a lifetime.

Many of the cowboys seemed happy to talk. One I met called Randy Taylor spent his summers driving around the country on the rodeo circuit. His winters were spent at college studying to become a chiropractor – a useful thing to learn given the number of his colleagues nursing bad backs. I asked Randy how his fellow students regarded his summer job.

'They are a bunch of easterners and do not understand why I risk my body this way, and believe me I do know the risks. But I also know the rewards, and I am not talking about money.

'The trouble is that when people like me go to see a doctor the first thing they do is to tell us to give up rodeo. We don't want to hear all that shit, we just want to know the quickest way of getting back on to a bronc.'

I was still behind the chutes when the bull riding event started. This is really the biggest manifestation of insanity. Bronc riding can be justified because it grew up out of horse breaking – a necessary part of running any decent-sized ranch. But climbing on to the back of one and a half tons of bull is just plain stupid. A bucking bronc may stomp a man by accident but a bull is likely to turn and deliberately try to gore him. There are no pick-up riders to offer a soft landing and easy let-out. The only way off a bucking bull is to let go and fall off.

It is then that the rodeo clown starts to earn his money. His job is to offer himself as a more tempting target than the winded cowboy. At least the rodeo clown is paid for his night's work – around five hundred dollars. The cowboy is usually paying to risk his life.

The tension behind the chutes rose a notch or three. I could only try to understand what it was like – to climb down into that chute, to feel the hot bulk of the bull between your legs with that massive neck stretching out in front, knowing that the only way off was to fall off. Bull riders also have a leather strap to hang on to but it is fitted with bells to add to the annoyance for the bull. The rodeo contractor was there to supervise the operation. I noticed that he was using an electric cattle prod on the bulls, giving them one or two jabs with it before the gate was opened. Then at the signal for the off he gave the bull a third shock in the rump to ensure that it went out into the arena rather than tried to lose its rider in the chutes. The practice of using the prod on the bulls is not really allowed but clearly its use is now common practice.

The cowboys seemed happy to talk to the 'limey from the BBC'. They were not the bunch of farm boys I had expected. Several were from the city and clearly knew less about ranching and cattle than I did. They could cling on to the back of a bucking bull or horse but could no more rope or doctor a cow than the average New York taxi-driver. Several claimed to be working their way through college. There was a healthy rivalry between the bull riders and the ropers. The latter were much reviled and regarded as the prima donnas of the rodeo world with their ten-thousand-dollar horses and fancy clothes. They wore gloves to keep their manicured fingernails clean. The ropers, for their part, dismissed the bull riders as being a bunch of 'gristle heads' – a title the bull riders were rather proud of.

They invited me to join them in the bar they were going to that night. A group of us climbed into the back of a ten-year-old Chevrolet pick-up and headed into town. They hooted and whistled at the girls leaving the rodeo grounds. Two girls accepted the shouted invitation to join us and jumped into the back with us.

The bar was packed with bodies. At least half the people there were wearing cowboy hats – the straw ones which are the uniform of the west in the summer. The air was full of country music and cigarette smoke. The people on the dance floor were doing the cowboy jive, the girls with their tight jeans and long hair swinging into and out of their partners' arms.

The rodeo cowboys made me welcome in their midst – as welcome as they could. But I was from an alien culture. There was an unbridgeable gap between us. Not just because I was English, not just because I spoke funny and came from a different culture, but because I had never ridden a bull. I had not been through the initiation ceremony.

I asked them why they did it but finding words that could contain and describe the experience was not easy. One of my new friends told me that riding a bull was better than sex.

'Right now I feel great. I have looked death and injury in the face and I have survived.·I have risked my body and I still have it. I can move my legs, my arms, it feels great. Before I climbed on to that bull I was terrified, now the adrenalin rush is over and I feel great. I am going to get drunk with my friends, try to find a girl and get laid.'

Another told me that unless he gets scared witless – he used another similar-sounding word – at least once a week he does not feel as though he is alive. He admitted to being an adrenalin junky – no better and no worse than a sky-diver or bungy-jumper. I had assumed that these young men were a group of no-hopers, merely a group of farm boys taking this one and only opportunity at the big time.

I think that at that moment, if the opportunity had been there, I would have climbed down the chutes on to one of those monstrous bulls and taken the risk. Gone for that ride so that I could become one of them, join their society, take down that barrier between us. I wanted to be a rodeo cowboy, to travel the length and breadth of America in my pick-up truck, sleeping in cheap hotels or with loose women and become a man.

But when the morning and the hangover came I remembered that I was an Englishman, a husband, a father and a coward.

13

Hog calling, Sam Peckinpah and a miffed giraffe

She had a 'volumptuous' figure, blonde hair and thighs purpose-built for powering the pedals of a bike. Her name was Patty but by the time her soft American 't' had got to her name it came out as Paddy. She was the proprietor of Cycle Sport in North Platte and she told me that I must be mad, bad or sad to even contemplate cycling the seven hundred miles from North Platte to Pocatello in Idaho.

'You cannot possibly realise what it will be like. Wyoming is boring. It is seven hundred miles, uphill, against the wind, across some of the most tedious scenery in the country,' she said. Patty asked me if I had done much cycling at home in Britain. I said that I had a three-speed bike with a wicker basket on the front. I ride it twice a year, whether I need the exercise or not.

She told me that North Platte was at about 3,000 feet and that I would be pedalling up to around 11,000 feet.

'You will be cycling beside the world's longest railway grade. Thirty-five miles of continuous uphill, without a break,' she said.

Once she realised that I was not going to be talked out of the venture she broached the delicate question of how much I was prepared to spend. I told her that a hundred dollars was my absolute limit. She sighed. Then she sighed again. She said that she had nothing in my price range.

'Nothing at all, not second hand?' I said.

She sighed again. She was rather good at it. She handed me the telephone and dictated the number of her rival bike shop in North Platte. The man on the other end of the phone laughed at me. On balance I preferred Patty's exasperated sighs to derision. I asked her if there were any other places I could buy a cheap bike. She got the keys to her truck, told her husband to mind the shop and she drove me down to the pawn shop. There were half a dozen bikes there. Only one had a frame big enough for my six-foot frame. She looked it over, she tutted. It cost 110 dollars. I would have paid up but Patty did not think that it would make the trip. She said that she would not send her worst enemy around the block on a bike like that.

We went down to the shopping mall to a big department store where she said I could buy a really cheap new bike for 130 dollars. I hardly noticed that she had edged me above my hundred-dollar limit, not once but twice. Clever woman. As we drove into the mall car park, a crowd was watching a man standing on a wooden box. He was screaming at a microphone. He was grunting and shouting 'Sweet, sweet, sweet.' The crowd gave him a tremendous round of applause. His place was taken by a woman who made an even more uncivilised noise.

Patty told me that it was a hog-calling contest. There were no pigs to be seen. The judging was being done by a panel of judges who were supposed to sit there and think like a pig. Patty seemed unable to give me a good explanation as to what makes a good hog-caller.

We walked into the bicycle section in the chain store. We looked at the shiny new bikes which I could have bought for 130 dollars. She bustled, she span wheels to see if they ran true, she prodded the seats. She sighed a bit. Patty said that she would not send her worst enemy across Wyoming on a bike like this. She laughed, then said she would.

I found myself asking her what she could find for me at

150 dollars. Yet again my upper limit had moved upwards.

When we came out of the store the hog-calling had stopped and a group of cowboys were throwing members of the public into a big tank of cold water. Patty told me, in a shockingly matter of fact way, that the people were getting a dunking for not wearing a minimum of three items of western wear.

Then a play of sorts started up. It was a simple plot about a quack doctor who stole some money from the bank. It was all good clean family entertainment – but with a great deal of gunfire during which three-quarters of the cast died violent deaths. It was as though someone had invited Sam Peckinpah to direct an amateur production of *Aladdin*.

Patty fixed me up with a bike. It was a slim Japanese job with ten gears. I wished that it could have been British. She agreed to put a luggage rack on it but did not like it when I insisted on mudguards. Proper bikes have mudguards – without them you get a terribly undignified skid mark up the back of your trousers.

I paid slightly over the 150 dollars by the time the extras were included. As I cycled away I was not sure whether Patty was an extremely nice person or a brilliant sales-woman. In America it is possible to be both. I left Patty my address and told her to call in when she cycled from Lands End to John O'Groats.

North Platte was still asleep when I left early on the Monday morning. Patty had advised me to start as early in the morning as I could before the heat started to build up and the wind started to blow. It had seemed too easy to get on the bike and go. It did not need catching, feeding, brushing or saddling. I just got out of bed, packed up, prodded the tires and started pedalling. Perhaps this cycling would not be all that bad after all. I started out along the hard shoulder on Highway 30. This kept me well out of the traffic but the bike clonked over huge, unfilled expansion joints. With every jolt the bicycle saddle became more intimate with the delicate parts of my bottom. I had hoped that the horse riding would have toughened my backside but I soon realised that a bicycle seat can penetrate to places a horse saddle can only dream about reaching. I tried steering around the biggest crevasses but this proved to be fruitless. In the end I moved across to the road proper and hoped that the trucks and cars would move across to avoid me.

As I pedalled along I thought about my plans and decided that I had a one hundred to one chance of them working out. Only a hopeless optimist would expect them to come out right. I remember being told about a farmer leaning disconsolately on a gate looking at his crop of hay which has just been rained on for the third time.

His neighbour sees him there and tells him to cheer up, 'That is what life is all about, win some, lose some.'

The farmer looks across at his neighbour and says, 'Gee, that would be great.'

I subscribe to the idea that whatever can go wrong will go wrong and that a good plan is almost as likely to come unstuck as a bad one. There was plenty of scope for things to go seriously awry over the next three weeks. The horses were to stay at the Buffalo Bill Ranch for another three weeks. Then someone I had never met was going to pick them up and truck them the seven hundred miles across Wyoming to be dropped off at the county show ground at Pocatello, Idaho. I had paid a farrier a hundred dollars cash up front to shoe the horses before they left the ranch. They and I would arrive in Pocatello about the same time as the wagon train. I would then finish the remaining 750 miles with the wagons – assuming that they were still rolling.

The plan had any number of weak links but the weakest of all was the bit about trucking the horses. I was beginning to think that I had been really stupid.

Two days earlier I had cycled over to the killer horse plant in North Platte and asked where the truckers usually go to eat. I think the man on the gate thought that I was up to no good, at best a pimp, at worst a drug dealer. Even a long explanation of my mission failed to persuade him that I was embarking on a genuine quest. In retrospect, I can hardly blame him for disbelieving me.

At the café I was given the phone number of a trucker who made a regular run into North Platte from eastern Idaho. He was usually running empty on the return trip. I phoned him up and the voice on the other end of the telephone said that for one hundred dollars in cash, no questions asked, none answered, he would pick my horses up from the Buffalo Bill Ranch and drop them off across the border in Idaho. He promised to pick them up in three weeks' time. The trip across Wyoming would take less than a day.

As I cycled along fresh doubts about my wisdom began to creep in. If the trucker turned out to be dishonest he could drop them off at the North Platte slaughterhouse and pocket six hundred dollars for each of them. I would not find out whether I had been right to trust the man until I cycled into Pocatello in three weeks' time. By then Rocky and Roland could be neatly parcelled up into freezer packs and well on their way to a rendezvous with a French dinner table. If I had been swindled I did not fancy my chances of getting any compensation. As the trucker had said, it was strictly a cash deal; no questions asked, no questions answered. I spent quite a few miles thinking about the reaction I would get from the unfortunate Pocatello policemen who had to listen to my tale of woe. I imagined the look of increasing disbelief on his face as he typed in the details of my complaint. I doubted whether it would be possible to find a lawyer who would help me out either – certainly not when he found out how stupid I had been.

As the miles rolled past my imagination began to take over. The trucker became a bigger and bigger ogre, the Idaho desk sergeant became more and more incredulous, the tears would start rolling down his ample cheeks, his double chin would vibrate with mirth as he called his colleagues over to hear about this stupid Englishman. The Pocatello papers would get hold of the story and I would finish up as one of those funny 'and finally' items at the end of the television news.

However, as Oscar Krause had said six weeks before, the only way to find out if someone is trustworthy is to trust them. My fevered brain worked over the terrible possibilities. Oscar's philosophy began to seem positively foolhardy.

After travelling at the sedate three miles an hour of a walking horse it felt as though I was really flying along on the bike. The trees whizzed past at ten miles an hour. The perspectives on buildings, irrigators and electricity pylons changed by the second. I could see why the bike was considered such an advance over the horse. It took me less than an hour and a half to make the thirteen miles to Hershey. I stopped at a garage and bought a coffee and felt pretty pleased with myself. I had intended to stop at a small town called Sutherland for breakfast but decided to push on to a place called Paxton – home of the famous Ole's Big Game Lounge and Grill. I had been told that I should not miss this particular watering-hole. I made such good progress that I got there before they opened up.

Ole could not have been all that popular with a depressingly large number of animals. The walls and ceiling of the bar are lined with hundreds of stuffed heads and several complete animals. The record book has it that the first dead animal arrived in Ole's bar in 1938. It was a humble deer. Ole basked in the admiration of his customers. He spent the next thirty-five years looking for more and more bizarre creatures to shoot. He shot one of almost everything America had to offer before turning his attention further afield. I had been told that Ole had even gone to Scotland to do some shooting. He was disappointed with the size of the deer but he thought that the Highland cattle with their impressive horns and cute fringe would look good on his wall. He bought one from a farmer and shot it in the field. I could not see any sign of the Highland cow in Ole's bar so perhaps the story was untrue.

The end wall of the bar almost supports the head of a down-in-the-dumps elephant and a slightly miffed giraffe. Both are so big and heavy that they have been wired to the ceiling to prevent them from drooping. In between the stuffed heads are hundreds of pictures of Ole with various dead animals and, behind a wrought-iron fence, there is a small tableau of a mountain lion bringing down a deer. A polar bear has pride of place in a glass case by the front door.

I read the leaflet on the table while I waited for my breakfast: 'Paxton, Nebraska, boasts a population of 550 of the friendliest people to be found anywhere, all equally proud of the museum quality of Ole's astounding collection of fish and game. Many are willing to share their own versions of the adventures of their home town living legend.'

Neither the people of Paxton, nor Ole, were much in evidence. The place did have a museum feel to it but whether you would want to eat breakfast in a museum I do not know.

'Whether you need to wet your whistle, partake of Nebraska's corn-fed beef, enjoy a game of billiards, tour the lounge or sit around and soak up some of the atmosphere . . . it's a stop you won't soon forget.'

One phrase in the leaflet stuck in my mind and brought it home to me that even the Nebraskans think of their state as one to pass through rather than to visit: 'Travelling through Nebraska without visiting Ole's Big Game Lounge is comparable to touring Yellowstone National Park without visiting Old Faithful.' Notice that you pass through Nebraska but you visit Yellowstone.

I tried to soak up the atmosphere. I decided that it had the atmosphere of a morgue. It was as dead as the animals lining the walls. But then it was just gone eight on a Monday morning so perhaps I was not giving the place much of a chance. I wondered whether I would like Ole and decided without ever meeting him that I would not.

By lunchtime I had completed my fifty miles and arrived at a place called Lake McConaughy. The lake is twenty-five miles long with the sort of white sandy beaches and blue water I have only ever seen in pictures of the Caribbean. The map showed a dozen places where camping was permitted – they were all nearly deserted. I thought of the summer traffic jams around Lake Windermere in Britain and realised what a terribly crowded island I live on.

I considered carrying on but decided that it would be better to build the miles up fairly slowly, so I stopped at one of the camp sites. By two o'clock in the afternoon I had been for a swim and was sitting at a picnic table in the shade with a nice cool westerly breeze blowing. In one morning on the bike I had travelled the same distance as would have taken me two and a half days with the horses. I thought that I stood an extremely good chance of catching the wagon train. I had failed to get the horses to Oregon without cheating but at least I would get there by muscle power.

Nebraska is usually flat, sometimes it is rolling, but not often. The trip from North Platte to Scotts Bluff was about 150 miles. I was following the river so it was steadily uphill – although I climbed a mere 1,000 feet the whole way. It would not be noticeable in a car but I thought I could detect it on the bike. The trip took me three days; it would have taken me ten on the horses.

Nebraska is a good place for cycling, or it would be but for the wind. Cycling against the wind feels much the same as cycling uphill except that hills have tops and the reward of coasting down the other side. On day trips on a bike you can expect to have the wind behind on the way home – although it seldom is – but in the prairies the wind blows from the west and almost nowhere else. If you should ever consider cycling across the United States I strongly recommend that you travel west to east.

I spent most of each day in a travelling trance, listening to the rhythms of my own body – my heart, my lungs, my legs. I stared with fascination at the tarmac road surface being pulled under my front wheel to disappear behind me. I only took in the scenery when I stopped to rest my legs and to re-establish some sort of blood flow to my bottom. Then I would contemplate the countryside and notice that it was changing around me from the precision neatness of irrigated cornfields to the freer forms of cattle land. Fences, some neat, some messy, started to appear. There were even a few rocks to be seen in the pastures. I was travelling along the north side of the Platte river while the trail went along the south side. Eventually the land became sandy, with strange grass-covered dunes. It felt as though the sea must be getting closer, which was true – although it was still over 1,500 miles away.

I dropped into a routine of getting up as soon as it was light. I would get on my bike and ride until I came to a garage, where I bought coffee and a chocolate bar for instant energy and rotten teeth. I then cycled again until 8.30 or 9 a.m. when I would find a café for breakfast – the best part of the day.

I liked the ones with at least half a dozen tatty pick-up trucks outside. I am told that a police car is also a good sign, although I never really put that to the test. Mid-western farmers like to start the day with a trip into town for a cup of coffee and a good moan with their friends. The cafés have a large table set out for them all to sit at. Most wear peaked caps with the names of a tractor manufacturer or a hideously toxic pesticide printed across the top. A few wear cowboy hats, although they are mostly the older men. In the mid-west it is perfectly acceptable to wear a hat indoors. Jeans are compulsory. They are always too long in the leg so that they touch the ground behind the heel. They fray there first. Even those who never ride horses wear jeans and cowboy boots.

Few farmers carry guns around, although many will have a rifle in their pick-up. What they do have is a small leather holster at their waist which carries either a pair of mole grips, a half-inch spanner or an adjustable wrench. There must be a lot of badly mangled nut heads in the USA heartland.

The topics of conversation around the moaning table are usually rather limited. The number one and two slots are occupied by the government and the weather. They frequently change places, although the government usually enjoys pride of place. Number three is always taken up with the 'greedy bassards' in the agricultural supply industry. The reviled companies are usually the same ones whose logos appear on the farmers' hats. Other subjects under discussion include the banks, lawyers, the armed forces, environmentalists and communists. To all intents and purposes the last two can be regarded as being the same subject.

The farmers hardly ever buy breakfast at the café for fear that their neighbours will think that they are too affluent or, even worse, that their wives are unwilling to cook it for them. Despite this, they still like to drink and moan in places which would serve them a good breakfast if they wanted it. It is hard to believe that these cafés ever make any money – coffee was only twenty-five cents (about twenty pence). The level of conversation would drop as I entered and a few faces would look around to see the stranger who had come into their midst. But it was just curiosity, not malevolence. The fact that I was wearing shorts set me apart even more.

Americans seldom say please or thank you to their waitresses. They will walk in, look at the menu and say, 'I need bacon, eggs – sunny side up, hash browns.' Bacon is always streaky and cooked to a cinder, eggs are always eaten in twos. One morning I sat opposite a construction worker who expressed horror at the idea of putting mustard on bacon or sausages. He then proceeded to mash his eggs into his hash browns and drown the gooey mess in tabasco sauce. It looked as though he was eating a road casualty. Toast is always white and comes with grape jam. No one ever eats marmalade. Coffee is drunk black. If you ask for cream you are offered a small sachet of chemicals which turns the coffee white but has no other discernible effect except to make the coffee feel slightly greasy on the tongue. Americans have the world's biggest and best dairy industry yet they put chemicals in their coffee.

Southerners eat grits, which taste, and look, like ground-up corn-flake boxes, while the mid-westerners eat 'biscuits and gravy' for breakfast. These are scones covered in a white sauce. Sometimes a few tiny flakes of mushroom are thrown in, making the sauce look as though it has been cooked in a pan which was not quite clean. But for real artery-clogging calories, the plate-size pancakes covered in butter and syrup are hard to beat. You may die young but you will go with a sticky smile on your toothless face.

Cyclists are not that common in America. It is the land of the motor car and people who choose to ride a bike in the mid-west are regarded as being slightly dotty. When I shifted from horses to bike, my social standing plummeted. No one stopped to talk to me, although my accent was still a big advantage. As soon as I opened my mouth people wanted to talk to me, to find out what I was doing, but their attitude had changed. When I was travelling with the horses the people I met were completely taken with my quest, they were falling over themselves to get involved and to help me in any way they could. Now that I was on a bike there were no offers of help, advice or hospitality. I felt that it would be too much of a cheek to turn up on someone's door step and ask to be able to camp in their yard, so I sought out the anonymity of proper camp grounds. I ate at cafés and fast food places. I got a shower most nights.

My changed lifestyle meant that I was starting to see a different sort of America. Until I transferred to the bike, I had been meeting farmers, park rangers and rural postmen. Now I was mixing with the people who take to the road for their work, their holidays, retirements and even their whole lives. They hit the road in conventional caravans towed by vans or cars; or they use campers which are slotted into the back of a pick-up truck. Many of them use giant motorhomes – often the size of conventional single-decker buses. These always have a small car in tow because the bigger motorhomes are impossible to get around shopping centres.

The vehicle of the moment is a giant fifth-wheel caravan. Instead of being hitched to a tow bar on the back of a truck, these monster trailers are attached to a special frame in the middle of the truck-bed. They are like mini articulated lorries. The trailers are as big as the motorhomes but when you get to your camp ground, the truck can be unhitched and driven around without the immense bulk of the trailer attached. These caravans have a master bedroom in the overhang above the truck-bed, they have large kitchens, a second bedroom, a proper bathroom and full air-conditioning. The camp sites are designed to cope with such behemoths. Umbilicals supply water, electricity, sewerage and cable TV – offering a minimum of fifty channels.

One time when I was sitting at a truck stop having lunch, a motorhome with a pick-up truck in tow went past. Inside the back of a truck was a motorbike. I made a comment to the trucker at my table about it.

'Americans love to travel,' he told me, as he wiped burger juice from his lower lip. 'If we are moving we think we must be having a good time. Truckers think they have the best job in the world, because we are being paid to do what most people in this country do on vacation.'

About mid-morning of the third day I saw a slim pencil

of rock ahead of me. It was Chimney Rock – a 500-foot tall geographical aberration jutting out into the plains. From forty miles away it looked as though it had to be man-made. The books say that the people on the slower wagon trains watched this thing grow up out of the horizon for five days before they actually got to the spring of clean fresh water which bursts out of its base. It took me a good five hours of cycling against the wind before I got to it. At times the rock seemed to be getting further away – like a bad sequence in a dream. The emigrants were pleased to see the rock because it marked the end of the prairies and the start of a new phase of the trip through the mountains. I was looking forward to cooler nights but I wondered whether my legs would be up to the task ahead.

When seen close up, the Chimney is an incredibly narrow column of yellow rock jutting out into the sky from a conical base of scree. It is an impressive example of the way that God will occasionally do something entirely un-expected with His planet – just when you think you are getting the hang of a place he goes and throws in a one-off like Chimney Rock. Had my legs not been made of jelly after a day of cycling into the wind, I think that I might have walked up to the rock to give it a pat. But even geo-graphical aberrations can be less attractive than a nice shower and a good night's rest.

I found a good camp site at Scott's Bluff. It was right beside the freeway and the railway so it was rather noisy but it had good showers, a swimming pool and was handy for Pizza Hut. In the shower room at the camp ground I met a man from Washington State. He was shaving and as I stood beside him with my chin covered in froth we had a long conversation out of the corners of our mouths.

He was with a party of thirteen people travelling in a large motor-home. Five adults and eight children. They had been right the way across to New York and were now on their way back home. By the end of their three-week holiday, they would have driven 7,500 miles – that is 300 miles a day. Their motorhome did about seven miles to the gallon – that is 1,000 gallons of fuel. I asked him if they were still friends after having spent all that time cooped up in the motorhome.

'Yes, I think we are – but we are Jehovah's Witnesses. I guess you could say that we leaned pretty hard on the bible.'

Other people I met thought nothing of driving five thousand miles during a two-week holiday – and many working people only get two weeks' holiday. To live in America and not get to see the best parts of this great country would be a terrible sin, even if that means spending most of your vacation on the road. But sometimes the travel lust takes over. Several of the campers or trailers have large maps of the United States stuck on the side. Their owners colour in the states they have visited. An unbelievable number claim to have visited every one of the fifty-two states in the Union. The trouble is that you hear people saying things like – 'Yuh, I been to Idaho, we drove through there in '71.'

Colour it in on the map, honey.

14

Pretty Boy, Kermit, sore heads and sarsaparilla

The next day I crossed the border into Wyoming and cycled into the town of Fort Laramie. The sun was high overhead. My bike-riding shadow looked black against the white of the street. The official road sign marking the town limit said: 'Fort Laramie, home to 250 good people and six sore heads.' It is inconceivable that a British parish council would put its collective insanity on show in such a way. The locals in the café at Fort Laramie informed me that the signs had been up for several years – long enough for them to have needed refurbishment at the tax payers' expense. Not one of them thought that the joke was wearing a bit thin.

The town of Fort Laramie has a couple of bars, a junk shop masquerading as an antique shop, a small general store, a school and a trailer park. The junk shop is run by a Bohemian old lady called Joyce Collins, who looks as though she would be happier in Greenwich Village or Highgate than marooned in a sea of farmers in mid-America. Joyce favours flowered blouses and fawn slacks as covering for her ample body. She has a degree in fine art and gave up being a potter when she turned sixty. These two pieces of information were slipped easily into the first two minutes of our conversation.

Joyce shares her life with a gargantuan shaggy mongrel which she calls Pretty Boy. He arrived on her doorstep five years ago. She heard him barking outside her front door, opened it and said, 'Oh, what a pretty boy.' He wagged his tail and got stuck with the name. It does not seem to bother him much.

She said that Pretty Boy had been thin and over-sexed. Joyce lavished love and fattening delicacies on him until he was no longer thin. She then took him down to the vets to have something irrevocable done about his libido. She told me that 'he is a much happier dog . . . now'. His desire to fight or fornicate with the other dogs of Fort Laramie is a distant memory. Pretty Boy offers his ponderous and amiable greeting to every human being who comes into the shop.

Joyce's shop is a jumble of junk, an amorphous pile of paraphernalia. Wooden ladder-back chairs, occasional tables and ugly ceramics share space with other less identifiable items. One is an old butter churn. Joyce told me that it had been designed and built by a man for a woman to use. Female right arms had to be strong a hundred years ago. Joyce's definition of an antique is something that your grandmother threw out. However, she also sells car registration plates from 1970. Technically they fit her description because they are the sort of thing my grandmother would have thrown out . . . as soon as the new 1971 plates were issued. Joyce also has a few bits of pottery – milk jugs and vases which she sells for no more than thirty dollars. She has trays of stones and river-polished pebbles which she hopes to sell for a dollar a piece. The pebbles were bought from a couple of local tramps who live down by the river.

'The poor fellows looked hungry and I wanted to help them,' she says. It was a good job she did not treat them exactly the same way she treated Pretty Boy.

Customers explore the dusty recesses of the shop by themselves, left to enjoy the pleasures of unearthing the treasures on their own. In one corner there is a wooden construction which looks like a high-backed commode with coat hooks on the back. She claimed it came from the old Fort Laramie itself. It used to grace her own front hall – until one thanksgiving dinner her two sons started arguing about which would inherit the stand when Joyce slipped her mortal coil. She thought that it was a bit rich to conduct the argument in front of her and at her own dinner table as though she had already popped her clogs. She said she would sell the damn thing. So there it is in the shop. I looked at the price tag – $2,500.

'That'll teach 'em,' she said with a smile.

It has been there for three years. Joyce has priced it so high that no one will ever buy it. Every time her sons have an argument she threatens to reduce the price on the commode. They no longer bicker about it in front of her.

Fort Laramie, the wild west fort proper, is three miles from town and Joyce Collins' antique shop.

Fort Laramie. The name haunts a thousand western films and a score of television series. The mental image is unequivocal – a wooden palisade with wooden towers on each corner and gates which swing back to admit a single arrow-riddled soldier who falls off his sweating horse seconds after entering the safety of the compound. In later scenes, mounted Indians fire flaming arrows into the timbers as the soldiers inside fight to save their lives.

The reality of the western fort could not have been more different. Some did actually have wooden palisades but they were outside the main fort complex. They were used for keeping livestock safely out of reach of light-fingered locals. The real defence of the fort lay in the numbers of heavily armed men who lived there. The Indians would never have risked making a frontal attack on the place. They might have made a sneak attempt to steal a few horses – hence the corral – but why attack the fort when its supply wagons were a much easier and more lucrative target?

The centre of Fort Laramie is a grassy parade ground with a dozen or more comfortable western houses around it.

They are painted white for neatness and to reflect the prairie sun. Balconies ring both the upper and ground floors. It was here that the officers, chaplain and surgeons lived in some comfort with their wives. The enlisted men lived in block house barracks – safely out of smelling distance of the officers' houses. During the winter the fort would have been ringed by a long, curving stack of firewood. The logs were kept away from the buildings to minimise the fire risk, not to provide a defensive line. Come April the circle of logs would have been completely burned up.

Now the fort is a quiet and remote tourist attraction. There is a book shop, a café, a bar where a jolly man with handlebar moustaches serves sarsaparilla in souvenir bottles. The bottles are much nicer than the contents, which taste like an unfortunate blend of cough mixture and diet coke. The buildings are decorated as they would have been in the fort's heyday in the 1870s. The officers and their wives seemed to have had it pretty good. The barrack blocks where the enlisted men lived looked less than comfortable. The shortage of women and comfort for the enlisted men guaranteed that many of them deserted to join the wagon trains which came through Fort Laramie each spring.

Every mid-day, during the tourist season, four men dressed in blue army uniforms from the 1870s discharge a field gun. The leader of the gun crew was a schoolteacher. In the USA teachers are seldom paid a salary during the summer months; they are expected to find alternative means of employment. Forty years ago this particular teacher's parents made a dreadful mistake – they decided to name him Kermit. They could not have known that he would have to share the name with an animated frog. I explained that Dylan is a marijuana-smoking rabbit in a children's programme on British television. Kermit felt that for the first time in his life he had met someone who could sympathise with his problem.

Kermit explained to the crowd of 'gee honeys' that the Howitzer was designed to be broken down into pieces to be carried on the back of mules. It was employed by the army for its psychological rather than its military effect. Such artillery was pretty useless against Indians who believed in guerrilla warfare. A hard steel ball could be used to knock out the defences of a fort – the Indians had no forts. The guns could be loaded with grape-shot and used to good effect against a tight formation of infantry – the Indians rode into battle in loose groups. The Sioux soon worked out the range of such field-pieces and stayed outside it until the guns had been discharged. They would then dash in towards the soldiers, hoping to get there before the men managed to reload with grape-shot. The range was about 250 yards. A good gun crew can fire four rounds a minute. A good horse can sprint at forty miles an hour – covering 265 yards in fifteen seconds. The Indians would be hoping that they were up against a slow gun crew; the soldiers would be hoping that the Indians had slow ponies. Warfare is full of inexorable and disgusting logic.

On a good day Kermit and his crew can manage two rounds per minute. This was not a good day for them. Kermit pulled the friction primer and the gun failed to go off. He and his four men stood around looking sheepish. They stood frozen to the spot in case the gun should still decide to go off. It did not. Kermit reinserted the friction primer and gave it another good tug.

And again.

The third time he hit pay dirt. He and his men would have been thoroughly overrun.

I met a park ranger called Becky Isenbath. She was tall, over forty and had big round glasses. Her wide-brimmed hat, olive-green skirt, khaki blouse and sensible shoes made her look rather severe but her humanity shone through in her quiet mid-western accent with its muted vowels and softened syllables. She changed my perception of the emigrants who took the Oregon Trail. Until then I had seen the pioneer emigrants as people engaged upon a great adventure – families which were grabbing a new life for themselves and their children. Becky told me that I was wrong. A few might have been on the trail for the pure adventure of it but for the rest it was a different story.

'Most of those emigrants were forced to sell up and go,' she said. The agricultural depression in the east was so great that the Mississippi paddle steamers were running on pig carcasses and grain because both were cheaper than wood or coal. In the late 1830s 'Oregon Societies' were formed in the towns along the banks of the Mississippi. Plans for heading west were made. People also wanted to escape the horrible middle-American winters and the scorching hot summers. The coastal strips promised mild winters and moderate summers. There would also be an escape from taxes. The farmers sold their properties for whatever they could get and then headed on west. To equip a family of five for the journey westward would cost a thousand dollars. That is a lot of money for a man to find – especially if an economic slump forced him to pack up in the first place.

The peak summers for emigration were 1850 and 1852. Each one saw fifty thousand people selling up and moving on west. There must have been many sad departures. People were leaving their families forever. They knew that they would never see their parents or brothers or sisters again. The emigrants thought that they were escaping the cholera epidemics of 1849 – but they found cholera all along the trail. Many of the women had to watch their menfolk die.

Becky told me that cholera strikes quick and hard. Within a couple of hours of first feeling queasy, the victim can have lost five gallons of body fluids through diarrhoea and sickness. The victim shrinks, eyes sink, skin wrinkles.

Over sixty per cent of the afflicted die. Becky told me that over half the deaths on the trail occurred in the first third of the trip, and most of those were from cholera.

Many of the families who arrived at Fort Laramie were in pretty poor shape. If they were running late like me, they may have opted to spend the winter at Fort Laramie. The Wyoming winters are formidable. The temperature falls to forty below zero — that is 40° Fahrenheit below zero or a full seventy degrees of frost — and the wind never lets up. The families may have arrived with a large number of live-stock — oxen, cattle, horses, sheep, mules. The animals may have been fairly safe from the Indians but there were other savages to deal with — white men. There were not many other places to go shopping. The stranded emigrants had to pay the prices on offer or go hungry. Then, as now, prices were fixed according to what the customer could afford. These customers were trading to save their lives.

'The people who over-wintered here at Fort Laramie would have done so because the journey was not going well for them. They would be the ones who arrived here in a poor state to continue the trip. You could be sure that they left here a good deal poorer than they arrived. This was a rip-off place,' Becky said.

She felt sorry for the emigrants. They were hoping for a better life but most of them found worse conditions in Oregon than they had left behind in the mid-west. They had moved to an area with nothing — virgin land which needed years of hard work to clear it of trees. The American government was the major stimulus for the migration west-ward. Oregon had to be filled with American citizens to stop the British, or even the Russians, from reclaiming it. The emigrants were the victims of government policy. Becky said that the emigrants' children may have benefited from the move across America — but those who made the trek probably regretted it until the day they died.

I asked Becky if she would have been one of those to

have made the trek, knowing what she does now. She told me that she would have done her best to dissuade her husband from his folly.

'Remember that the relationships between men and women were different then. In 1840 decent women always obeyed their husbands. If he had decided to go, then I would have had to pack up and go with him. You only have to read the trail diaries to know that many of the women thought the whole venture was a terrible mistake.'

Many of the women who went along the trail kept full diaries of the events of the trip. They knew that they were undertaking a journey that would have a profound influence on their descendants. I bought a book of their writings from the shop at Fort Laramie. They are often a dismal record of deprivation and disaster. Many start out with long flowery descriptions of the scenery, the people on the wagon train and the condition of the animals. Initially they have long reflective pieces about the deaths of people on the wagon trains. However, the diaries change as the trip progresses. Some women were traumatised by the whole experience and the diaries degenerate into a tally of the graves passed and miles made.

One was written in 1853 by a woman called Maria Parsons Belshaw who was travelling from Indiana with her husband:

> August 26: passed three graves, I dead horse, 18 cattle, made 13 miles.
> August 27: passed 5 graves, 1 horse, 23 cattle, made 15 miles.
> August 28: passed one grave, 17 cattle, made 23 miles.
> August 29: passed five dead cattle, made 15 miles.

The list goes on and on – a depressing catalogue which served no real purpose other than to shock an Englishman travelling the same route 150 years later.

I did not come across my first serious hills until after Fort Laramie. Then I had fifteen miles of climbing with dozens of false summits. I thought that I would never get to the top. I would have got off to walk but a cycle race was taking place. Huge mobs of racing cyclists came powering past me, onwards and upwards as though there was no gradient at all. My head was still full of Fort Laramie and the plight of the pioneer women. The cyclists with their phallic helmets and bright skin-tight lycra shorts seemed out of place amongst the subdued browns and yellows of the scenery. The cyclists made comments about snails or tortoises as they whirred on past me. They made me feel as though I were cycling in slow motion, like one of those dreams where you are the only one who is travelling through treacle. My white legs looked like pipe-cleaners compared to the polished mahogany limbs of the racers. My khaki shorts were ludicrously baggy – they had come to me after being discarded by an archaeologist I had met in Kansas. They would have looked baggy on the turf at Wembley in the 1948 FA cup final. I kept on cycling, fearful of the humiliation of walking while so many people powered past me up the hill. After the seventh false summit, exhaustion became a stronger force than humiliation and I got off to walk. I took the comments with a stiff upper lip.

I finally reached the real summit and cruised down the other side. The racers kept on overtaking. They seemed to be pedalling as hard going downhill as they had going up. Where on earth is the pleasure in that?

My map suggested that I would have to cycle along the side of Interstate 25 most of the way to Casper in Wyoming – about a hundred miles of motorway. I was not looking forward to it at all. However, I had forgotten what a large country America is. In Britain a road cannot be widened or improved without inflicting months or even years of misery on the existing traffic. Diversions and contra-flows mean that life is going to get much worse for the unhappy commuter before it gets better. In America, well in Wyoming anyway, they simply build the new road beside the old one. I found that I had to do very little cycling on the Interstate. The old Highway 26 was a little rough in places – sometimes almost craggy, like an old person's face – but I had both lanes pretty much to myself apart from the occasional local screaming along in a pick-up truck.

I arrived safely in Casper, the biggest city I had been in since leaving Kansas. It had traffic lights, banks, an endless number of bars. I bought my first frozen yoghurt, which tasted like ice-cream but had only a third of the calories. Frozen yoghurt, diet coke, sweetener – the American dream of indulgence without paying the penalty. I would have lingered in Casper much longer than I did had I known what I faced over the next week or so of cycling.

It was the stretch from Casper to the Idaho border which was so bizarre. In some ways the scenery is wonderful. Much of the trip, was across a wide rolling plain of the meanest cattle pastures you could imagine. The road ahead can be seen for twenty or thirty miles, dropping into and out of sight and changing course for reasons now long since forgotten.

The horizon is blocked by bald red mountains which somehow never seemed to get any closer. I wanted to take pictures but no camera in the world can do justice to the space and the perspectives. The lens confines, contains and subdues a view so vast it cannot be seen other than with the naked eye. The low humidity makes the air clear and clean, making a nonsense of guesses about distance.

I met a trucker in a café who told me about two of his colleagues who were travelling across Wyoming. They started talking about when to stop for supper. One said that it would be best to wait until they got to the mountains they could see ahead of them.

'We will be there in less than an hour.' His mate said that the mountains were much further than an hour away, they would not be in them until later that evening. The two men started arguing about the distance.

It became important to resolve the disagreement sooner rather than later. They saw an Indian sitting at the side of the road and decided to stop and ask him how far it was to the mountains. The truck hissed to a stop, one of the truckers leaned out of the window and shouted down to the Indian, 'Say bub, how far is it to them mountains?' He got no reply. He asked again. Still no reply. Cursing the intransigence and unhelpfulness of native Americans, the two truckers drove on. They did not arrive in the mountains until lunchtime the next day. One trucker turned to the other and said, 'Guess we were further away from that Injun than we thought.'

I felt as though I could cycle for three days with my eyes fixed on the road ahead of my front wheel, then look up and not be able to see that anything had changed. Perhaps in a car the mountains slowly move and change perspective but on a bike they are essentially static. I might as well have been sitting on an exercise bike and staring at a picture on the wall. I felt like an ant crawling through one of those Japanese gardens made of boulders and raked gravel.

The main vegetation is sage brush – a grey waxy waist-high shrub which likes to keep six feet of bare soil between it and its neighbour. The leaves are small and mean, the trunks twisted and tortured by the hard winters and tough summers. Some people actually like sage desert; they find it attractive enough to write poetry about it. They find it peaceful. I come from a country which is green and wet. At home you have to fight to keep soil bare of vegetation. You have to rake and weed and hoe it. Turn your back and it goes green within a month. Plants are queuing up to come and live there. In the Wyoming sage brush desert there is nothing which wants to live between the sage bushes. Just bare, inert soil. I understood why Americans call it dirt.

Then there were the flies. As long as I kept cycling it was fine but as soon as I stopped they turned up in droves to eat me. I wondered what they ate when I was not there.

I was pleased that I was not travelling alone with the horses. It would have taken me a couple of months to make the trip. I would be fearing for my sanity and the condition of the horses. I am sure that the locals would have helped me but there did not seem to be all that many of them around. The grazing for the horses would have been terrible. Judging by the look of the cattle it could not be particularly nutritious stuff to eat. I wondered about the state of the emigrant stock after weeks of travelling through this uncompromising scenery.

At night I turned to the radio for company. The dials were almost completely empty from top to bottom of all three bands. On several nights I could get just one country music station – I have never been a fan. I started to compile my own personal list of country and western all-time wrist-slashers. There is 'Love on the Rocks' and 'The Emptiest Arms in the World'. A particular favourite of mine was called 'Feed Jake'. It is about a dying man who thinks he might die before he wakes in the morning and makes a plea to his relatives not to forget to feed his dog Jake. Then there is one called 'Dear John': about a soldier who gets a letter from his girlfriend asking for all her pictures back because she has to tell him she has found another, dear John, I have to tell you it is your brother. Finally, my number one number is a dirge called 'Blood on the Saddle', about a rodeo star who dies in a great big puddle of blood on the ground.

As I cycled along I would occasionally glimpse a small grove of trees marking a wet spot in a pasture beside the road. I would make a point of stopping for a rest in the shade – for as long as the flies allowed. One time I fell asleep and woke an hour later: Still groggy, I climbed back on the bike and cycled on west. I saw ahead of me a truck

barrelling along on my side of the road. He saw me, flashed
his lights. I shifted across to the hard shoulder and gave him
the finger as he went past. I noticed that the driver was
sitting on the left hand side of his cab. It was me who was
on the wrong side of the road.

The days were hot and the nights were cool. I started
each morning wearing a sweatshirt and sometimes a coat.
By eleven I would be down to my T-shirt and baggy shorts.
I was using a factor 30 sun-blocker on my legs and
they were staying pearly white. One day I left it off and
burnt my legs badly. I had forgotten that I was well over
6,000 feet up.

I cycled through a modern ghost town called Jeffrey City.
It was a purpose-built home for the miners who were going
to be needed to exploit the uranium reserves in the area.
But the combined blows of the Three Mile Island nuclear
disaster and the demise of the nuclear arms race meant that
the modern housing estates, bowling ally, school and shopping precinct are empty and boarded up.

For hours of cycling I would see no sign of life other than
that of the ribbon of road I was travelling. There were the
inevitable road kills along the verge – possums, skunks and
the occasional stinking and bloated deer with its delicate
matchstick legs bent at crazy angles by the impact with a
car. Often a few scattered lumps of automobile lay nearby.
In a seventy-miles-an-hour collision with a deer the
damage is not all one way. The most common vehicles to
pass me were the huge silver double-lozenges of the oil
trucks. One square driver's cab and two shiny tubes in hot
pursuit. The slipstream lasted for thirty seconds or more.

The horizon was often punctured by the 'nodding
donkey' of a low-yield oil well. These forty-foot-long
monsters nod their counterbalanced heads up and down – a
single ponderous stroke every four or five seconds as they
slowly suck the oil from its million-year refuge hundreds of
feet under the hot Wyoming scrubland. The precious black

liquid is pumped into holding tanks which are emptied on a regular basis by the giant silver oil trucks. I came to develop a nodding acquaintance with their drivers.

The road continued to climb to South Pass at around 7,500 feet. This was where I crossed the great divide. From here on in the rivers would be flowing westwards, although I had been warned not to expect it to be downhill all the way. The pass was not as spectacular as I had expected it to be. The people who planned the Oregon Trail were looking for the easiest routes. Had it not been for the road sign I would not have noticed that I was passing through a dip in the Rockies.

The scenery became ever more desolate as I moved on west. I stopped for the night at a place called Farson. It had a shop, a café, a petrol station and precious little else. It was hard to imagine why someone would choose this as a place to live or to set up a business.

One day the hills seemed steep and the wind was strong. I was pushing the bike as often as I was riding it. Every time I stopped to push the bike cars and trucks would stop to see if I was all right. Lots of people offered me a lift to the top of the next hill, the next town or even the next state. In a moment of weakness I accepted a lift and threw my bike into the back of a pick-up truck and travelled for six or seven miles while the farmer talked to me. I saved myself an hour of cycling but it also meant that I could not claim to have travelled the Oregon Trail by muscle power. I regret accepting that lift. I think I would like to go back and walk that stretch of road.

Assuming that I could remember where it was.

15

Road apples, suicidal skunks and the mystery of the guberif

I cycled into Cokeville in more hope than expectation of finding the wagon train. It seemed too much to expect that it would still be bang on schedule after over a thousand miles of some of the toughest travelling in the country. Cokeville is a typical Wyoming town which grew out of a cluster of houses sown between the road and the railway tracks. A small tree-lined square of grass served as a park. It had an impressive plastic extravaganza of a children's play area – the sort of investment in the safe pleasure of the next generation a British town five times the size would deem to be an unnecessary burden on the rates.

Cokeville is the sort of place where most people pass through rather than stop. Those who bother to halt there in the morning will find a truck-stop full of yawning truckers and a café full of moaning farmers. An evening visit will reveal that the yawning truckers have been replaced by another group of truck drivers busy yarning their endless tales of the road. The moaning café clientele will have transferred their elbows to the bar to continue their variations on that day's theme of agrarian discontent. There is also a small store where the cost of petrol and the distance from the big town govern the prices of American essentials – chewing tobacco, coffee, sweets, breakfast cereals, frankfurter sausages and bread with the chemical-endowed gift of eternal youth but no trace of either taste nor texture.

As I rattled through town I was pleased to see some tell-tale nuggets of manure or 'road apples' lying on the road. Reasons for optimism but by no means proof that a wagon train had passed through. I saw the rear view of a tightly jeaned woman walking down the street. She would have been better off wearing something less figure-hugging – a marquee perhaps. I squealed the bike to a halt beside her and she looked round with a look of surprise on her face – not for the first time I felt the absence of a bell on the bike. I asked her if she knew where the wagon train was camped. She stared suspiciously at my mouth.

'Whad,' she said. I knew that she had understood me, she just wanted time to think and to listen to my accent again. I was getting used to Americans staring at my mouth as though I had a speech defect. I suppose it is not every day that an Englishman on a bike breezes into town and starts asking questions about the whereabouts of a wagon train. Americans in New York, Miami or California are well used to talking to English tourists and dealing with their odd questions. In the mid-west an English accent in the flesh is still a terrible shock to them, something they have only ever heard on the television.

I repeated my request for information. She asked me who had told me that there would be a wagon train in Cokeville. There was an odd mixture of incredulity and sympathy in her voice. It was as though I had come into town and asked her where I might find the jackalope ranch. It was the sort of reaction I might have reserved for an American who breezed into my own village of Botolph Claydon declaring that he had just bought the place from a man he had met on the plane to Heathrow. She did not actually tell me that there was not a wagon train in Cokeville but her voice revealed that that was what she believed. She did not want to be the bearer of bad tidings so she directed me to the general store – as bars are not the best places to get honest answers.

I had little faith in finding the wagon train that night but the lady behind the counter said that it was here and had gone somewhere across the tracks. As half a continent lay on the other side of the tracks this was not the most precise set of directions I had ever been offered – but she said that I could not miss it.

Of course.

I bounced the bike across the railway and found a dirt road with many hoof prints embedded in the dust. I got off and walked along the track rather than risk my thin tyres on the dirt road. I was just beginning to wonder how far 'the other side of the tracks' the wagon train might have gone before setting up camp when the air was polluted with the throaty squawking of a mule. The solo was joined by a chorus of follow-up brays and hoots. Then I spotted a curved white canvas peering over the top of a wooden fence in a farmyard beside the track. I knew that I had found the wagon train which had become the focus of my journey for so many, many miles. The thought of the wagon train and being able to travel in company with other people had sustained me since things had first started going so wrong back in Kansas. I had looked forward to this moment so much. It was there like a taste in the back of the mouth. I felt terribly emotional – but then a Fairy Liquid commercial can reduce me to tears.

I wished that I could have had the pleasure of riding my horses into camp. Then the relief at having caught up with the wagon train would have been accompanied by a sense of triumph. I had met the wagon train people just before they left St Joseph back in May, before I had bought Rocky and Roland. Then they had doubted my ability to catch up with them on horseback. They had been right and I had been wrong – not exactly a lifetime first for me. I decided not to suffer the indignity of walking, so I risked a puncture by climbing back into the saddle of my bike and wobbling slowly into camp. In retrospect, it would have been more dignified to have walked.

To their credit, there was a refreshing absence of 'I told you so's' from the wagon trainers. In fact, they seemed impressed by the fact that I had managed to cycle across Wyoming. Almost as impressed as if I had done the trip all the way on horseback. I ignored the gentle hissing from my front tyre as we talked.

They were down to two wagons and five people on horseback – a dozen people in all. More a wagon trainlet than a wagon train – but it still seemed like quite a crowd to me. There were also half a dozen trucks and trailers associated with the venture. Their back-up facilities were impressive. The wagon master was a slight man with an impressive beard. He was called Jesse and came from a Tennessee town called Greenbrier. Americans nearly always tell you the name of their home town. It is announced along with the name: 'I am Jesse Aldridge from Greenbrier Tennessee', or 'I am Ray Redman out of Salem Missouri.'

A group of us sat in the shadow cast by a big horse trailer and swopped stories of our experiences on the trail. It was wonderful, and would have been perfect had the conversation and trail dust been washed down with a beer or two – but coffee was not a bad substitute.

It emerged that their journey had not been much easier than mine. The six wagons which had started out from St Joseph two and a half months before had hit some really bad weather. They had twenty-five consecutive wet days and were then hit by a tornado which rolled the wagons over and piled them up against a fence, 'like leaves in a breeze' said Jesse. Several wagons which were intending to make the whole trip decided that this was too far from being fun. They packed up and went home to face the neighbours – and that is a brave thing to do. It is strange how in our society to have tried to do something and to fail at it is regarded as a smaller achievement than not to have tried at all.

I had missed the first week of bad weather while still at

Kansas City getting my horses ready and having my wallet stolen. I was then travelling through the state of Kansas, some hundred miles further south than the wagon train, which was travelling right in the worst of the bad weather. Then, when the weather was really nasty all the way across the mid-west, I was stuck at Lake Clinton while Rocky and Roland were both off the road.

The wagon train faced the worst of it all, day in, day out, travelling into the teeth of the wind and rain. In Nebraska they picked up several new groups of travellers and at one time had as many as fifteen wagons snaking along the roads. However, most of these people were locals and knew all too well that Wyoming was going to be mind-numbingly boring and even more like hard work. They had all dropped out by the time the wagon train crossed the border into Wyoming – some promised to come back for the prettiest four hundred miles through Oregon.

The people on the wagon train offered me supper, which I gratefully accepted. Before we ate I went back into town to get washed in the rest rooms by the park. I bought an ice-cold pack of twelve cans of beer and offered it around my soon-to-be travelling companions. Not one of them accepted. I continued to press the beer on them, telling them to drink it before it got too warm, but there were still no takers. Every time a new person joined the group around Jesse's wagon they were offered beer by the hospit-able Englishman. I kept on scattering my conversation with yet more offers of beer. Still no one wanted it.

Eventually, Ray, the trail boss, asked me if I would like to come and look at his horse. It seemed an unusual offer but one which would have been impolite to refuse. As soon as we were out of earshot he informed me that this was a dry wagon train and that it was Jesse who had insisted that it should be that way. Ray explained that he and one of the outriders, Gene, were the only drinkers on the train. What people did in the privacy of their own campers and trailers was their affair but, in public at least, drinking was banned. For the last two hours I had been sitting beside the trailer of the abstainer-in-chief and attempting to turn it into a drinking establishment – Jesse must have been really impressed with the Englishman.

'Drink if you want to, but please be discreet about it,' said Ray.

We went back to join the people sitting around Jesse's wagon and I kicked the beer out of sight under my chair. It was not until after I had crawled into my sleeping bag that I remembered that the remains of the twelve-pack was still there. It was tangible evidence of my sin and insensitivity. I waited until the camp fell silent and sneaked out of the tent like a thief in the night to retrieve it.

I got up at 5.30 ready for an early start for the Idaho border but the wagon train people had been up long before me – their animals were already fed and they were tucking into their own breakfasts. Not for the first time I wondered how Rocky and Roland were faring. They should be leaving North Platte any day now. I had another three days of cycling to get to Pocatello. The wagon train would take just on a week to get there, which should give me time to get the horses ready to continue their trip west. So far so good. I had closed the gap on the wagon train and had made it across Wyoming.

After two and a half weeks on the bike the hills were less of a problem to either me or my legs. I could even walk normally at the end of a day's cycling. I felt pretty good about the way things were panning out and was looking forward to sharing my journey with people who shared a common goal.

I had left the high desert behind and it was being replaced with much better quality grazing land. I was still in the mountains but they were green and grey and unspectacular – the scenery reminded me of parts of Scotland. In the early morning I had to bundle up against the cold but I was hot and sweaty by ten o'clock.

The road seemed to be littered with an unusually large number of dead skunks. I began to wish that American skunks would choose somewhere other than Wyoming hills on which to commit suicide under lorries. Cycling uphill past a dead skunk is a profoundly unpleasant experience. Lungs are working at full capacity when this overpowering smell wafts across the road. With every breath it is sucked deep down into the finest chambers. It is hard not to gag. If you stop breathing the world soon starts to go fuzzy around the edges and dizziness sets in. If you get off to walk, then you just have to spend that much longer in the plume of stink – which can easily be fifty yards long. It is hard to feel sympathy for a dead skunk when it subjects the innocent passer-by to such an experience.

As I crossed the border into Idaho I cycled across a slogan which had been written on the surface of the road. It was written in three parts with fifty yards of tarmac between each. It said, 'DON'T BE . . . A . . . GUBERIF.' It must have been done by a very particular graffiti artist because the letters were distended upwards so that they looked perfectly normal when viewed from behind the wheel of a car – or from a bike come to that. A matching set was printed on the road surface for those leaving Idaho. I assumed that it had to have been created by an individual.

A guberif, a guberif. A chap can lose a lot of miles in a reverie trying to work out what a guberif might be. I had just decided that the graffiti was the work of a demented individual when I came across the same slogan again. He must have been a diligent yob.

I was still ruminating on the meaning of guberif as I cycled into the first town in Idaho. Butch Cassidy and the Sundance Kid relieved the bank at Montpelier of 7,000 dollars. It was a pretty good haul. Apparently they had arranged for fresh horses to be left at Cokeville where I had left the wagon train. They had ridden their first set of horses for over thirty-three miles, with the Montpelier posse in hot pursuit. The posse turned up in Cokeville on their tired horses to find that the Hole in the Wall Gang had taken all the fresh horses and left their own exhausted animals behind. The posse gave up the chase as a hopeless venture. I expect the horses were pleased.

As I cycled into Montpelier I saw a police car at the side of the road and stopped to ask about guberifs. The policeman said something about 'our damn fool Governor Cecil Andrews'. I took it that Mr Andrews did not get this particular policeman's vote. The disgruntled cop told me that guberif is firebug written backwards. It fits in with the other great Idaho slogans – 'Keep Idaho green' and 'Idaho is too great to litter.'

There is something else which is odd about Idaho. Each state in the Union has its own design of car tax plate. Wyoming has a bucking horse, Utah has an advert for its skiing industry. Other states proclaim themselves to be full of sunshine, or trees. Idaho is a great big state, 270 miles east to west by 400 north to south. It has mountains, lava formations, grassland, swamps, all sorts of wonderful natural resources including gems, oil and coal. Idahoans have an awful lot to be proud of, yet they choose to drive around with the unforgettable slogan 'famous potatoes' on both the front and rear of their cars. Even police cars.

I asked the policeman about the slogan. I expected another tirade about dum politicians but he told me that he could see nothing wrong with it at all. He suggested that I should find time to visit the World Potato Exposition at Blackfoot. I told him that I would be certain to do just that. At the time I thought I was lying.

Two days later I arrived in Pocatello, or Pocatella as many of the locals would have it. Americans often change the end of a place name to the 'a' sound. Missouri becomes Missoura. I phoned the trucker who was going to pick Rocky and Roland up. His wife told me that he was on his way to North Platte and would be back in two days. He was expecting to pick the horses up tomorrow. I rang the Buffalo Bill Ranch and warned them that he was on his way.

I had forty-eight hours to kill, where else to go but to the World Potato Exposition in Blackfoot, Idaho – a forty-mile round trip? At one time this would have been an unthinkable distance to cycle just to look at potatoes. But the cycle trip across Wyoming had produced profound effects on both my mind and my body. The World Potato Exposition was worth every mile.

Blackfoot is a small Idaho town which considers itself to be the potato capital of the world. The 'Exposition' is housed in an old railway station in the middle of town. They have a machine which gives a running commentary as it churns out French fries in the shape of the state of Idaho. It has the ugly high-pitched voice of a whining schoolboy. There is a huge hall of potato planting, harvesting and riddling machinery; a potato telephone, a clock which runs off the electricity created by wiring up two spuds, the world's largest potato crisp (about the size of a pizza) and you can buy potato fudge, potato cookies and potato ice-cream in several different flavours. I tried apple-pie-flavoured potato ice-cream – it will never catch on.

If you wish to take away something more tangible than the after-burn of potato ice-cream in your mouth, you can also buy some of the world's most tacky potato souvenirs. 'Spud Buddies', a series of soft potato toys which have been modelled into different characters, include one that looks like a dog and is called Rin Tin Tater, another like a baseball player called Babe Russet, a third of Wild Bill Hash Brown and a fourth which is dead with some tyre-marks across its middle. It is called Mashed Potato. I am told that the mashed potato road victim is their bestseller. Idahoans have a sense of humour which is all their own.

It was the first day that I had spent on the bike in a built-up area. Cycling may be green, quiet and healthy for the planet but for the town cyclist it is the antithesis of all three. By the end of the day I felt grimy on the outside and grimy on the inside. I felt that this sort of cycling was bad for my own personal ecosystem. I had hardly noticed the occasional truck in Wyoming – vehicles made a welcome distraction – but this incessant city traffic made my ears buzz and my brain ache with trying to keep out of trouble. I understood the constant look of anger you see on the faces of bicycle dispatch riders in London.

The trucker had promised to deliver the horses to the county show ground at 11 a.m. on Saturday morning. Sure enough, bang on time, a large cattle truck rolled into the grounds. It had the right name over the top and the right horses inside. Rocky and Roland were slightly thinner and a bit knocked around but they looked bright and alert as they jumped down out of the truck. As Oscar Krause had said, 'The only way of finding out if you can trust someone is to trust them.' I had trusted the trucker and he had delivered. I counted out his hundred dollars, he gave me the envelope with the border permits and vaccination details, and we shook hands.

My plan had worked out better than I could have hoped. I had cycled across Wyoming, I was right back on schedule and I had my horses in the right place at the right time. The envelope also contained a covering letter from Tom Morrison, the park ranger at the Buffalo Bill Ranch.

To whom it may concern or bother to ask:
These two horses are being transported from the Buffalo Bill Ranch State Historical Park in North Platte, Nebraska, to some place out west where they will once again join their owner, Dylan Winter.
Mr Winter has been attempting to retrace the Oregon

Trail, talking all the way. It is said that only Englishmen and mad dogs go out in the mid-day sun.

Mr Winter saw the elephant about the time he reached Fort Kearny and decided to leave his horses with us until they could regain their composure. We wish them well.

It is agreed that while the horses were here they obeyed all applicable laws, rules and regulations promulgated by the State of Nebraska or any agency thereof or by the United States of any agency thereof.

Fees for boarding shall be paid in cash at the rate ½ or 0.01 per cent to the park superintendent upon Mr Winter's return to North Platte, whenever that occurs.

I went off to spend a humiliating hour or four on the phone pleading with Pocatello farriers and their wives in an effort to persuade one of them to come out and shoe my horses on a Sunday morning. I got one in the end. It must be great to do a job where everyone is nice to you.

16

Pesticide shower, Missouri Foxtrotter and chewing tobacco

The wagon train rolled into the county show ground at Pocatello late on Sunday afternoon. The next morning I was woken just after five by the sound of the mules braying their welcome to the day. As I lay in my tent I listened to Jesse turning the air blue as he tried to ensure fair play with the buckets of feed. The sound of him cussing Joe, Sandine and Bull was to become my morning alarm call for the next two months. As Jesse continued to cuss his mules I realised that he was not really swearing at all. The strongest oath he ever used was to call one of his mules a 'son of a buck'. He just said it with such gravelly fervour that it sounded like bad language.

Two hours later we were all hitched up, saddled up and ready to roll. We were waiting for the police escort to arrive to see us safely out of the Pocatello city limits. I was riding Rocky and leading Roland. The pack was stashed in one of the support rigs. Although there were just the two wagons and half a dozen 'outriders', it felt like quite a crowd. The wagons had large flags fluttering from poles on each corner. Roland looked suspiciously at the dancing monsters but Rocky had been to enough rodeos not to be bothered by them.

On the stroke of 7.30 Ray asking if everyone was ready. He stood up in the saddle, waved his hat and shouted, 'Wagons ho'. Strange that. I had always thought that they said 'Wagons roll', but I was assured that 'Wagons ho' was the authentic version. The mules leapt forward in their traces, shoved their shoulders into the collars and started off. They were setting a cracking pace as we went through town and I wondered whether they would be able to keep it up all day. Rocky was walking as fast as he could go and Roland had to trot all the time to keep up.

I dropped in beside another horseman called Gene. He was dressed from head to foot in authentic western clothes – long boots, big black Stetson hat, jeans, waistcoat. He had a big handlebar moustache and rode a spotted Appaloosa horse called Ruby. The turquoise-beaded Indian-style choker around his neck looked rather out of place on a man who was over fifty.

I could not have chosen a worse person on the wagon train to use as a source of information on my travelling companions. Gene was almost monosyllabic. By the end of the morning's ride I had managed to discover that the whole trip had been dreamed up by a grandmother called Betty, a retired trucker called Ray and Jesse, who was a retired Ford motor car production-line worker. Jesse's wife Caroline drove the second wagon with the help of Paula, who had left her husband and family back in Missouri. Then there was Harold, a retired postman also from Missouri. He was the flag man and rode along at the back waving traffic on past the wagon train – but only if he was given the all-clear by Ray who was riding at the head. Gene had been with the wagon train since halfway through Nebraska and thought that he would stick with it all the way to Oregon City at the end of the trail.

The police escort stayed with us for an hour or so and then left us to fend for ourselves. Our route took us through mile after mile of the potato crops which brought such pride to the people of Idaho. It was a blistering hot day – close on 100° F. Occasionally we would pass close to an irrigator and we would get a beautiful blast of cooled air which had passed through the fine mist of water. When I spotted an irrigator which was throwing water over the road I stopped Rocky under it for a moment or two to let the delicious moisture play on us. Gene spoilt my pleasure by warning me that the farmers apply their crop-sprays in the irrigation water. I spent the rest of the day imagining that my skin was burning.

I swapped horses at lunchtime and tied Rocky to the back of one of the wagons where he walked along as though he had been doing it all his life. I rode beside Jesse's wagon and talked to him about mules. They are a cross between a special breed of giant donkey and a female horse. Jesse said that the donkey stallions willingly breed with horses but once they have been allowed to breed with a donkey mare most of them will refuse ever to service a horse again. Since Jesse told me that, I have asked several people and most confirm that it is true. Mules are a true hybrid between the two species and are always sterile – even though they come as male and female. The males have to be gelded just like a horse otherwise they have all the enthusiasm and bad manners which go with a stallion – but none of the ammunition.

Jesse told me in his quiet Tennessee drawl that mules are both tougher and more intelligent than horses. The trail boss, Ray, had two horses which he alternated from day to day. So did Gene. Harold only had one horse, Ringo, who had gone sick for a while back in Wyoming.

'Them old critters just ain't tough enough but my old mules just keep rolling on down the road,' said Jesse proudly. He said that I should have bought mules for the trip, then I would not have had to resort to the bicycle.

My two horses had benefited from their three-week holiday. I was sure that if I split the riding between the two of them they would be able to get me through to the end of the trail, which was just under a thousand miles away.

Jesse kept a pretty tight rein on his wagon train. We were

always under way by 8.00 in the morning – sometimes
7.30. If someone was not ready by the time Ray shouted
'Wagons ho' they would be left behind to catch up as best
they could. We always stopped for twenty minutes mid-
morning, an hour for lunch and another twenty minutes
mid-afternoon. We travelled at least twenty miles in a day –
sometimes we did as much as thirty. It was no wonder that I
had been unable to close the gap between us when I was
dawdling along by myself back in Kansas and Nebraska.

On most nights the wagon train stopped at small-town
parks or rodeo grounds. The locals would often get
together and lay on a barbecue or a 'pot luck supper' for us.
Local horsemen or wagon drivers would come out and ride
with us for a few miles, a few hours or even a few days.

Within four days of leaving Pocatello our modest little
wagon train increased in size when we were joined by a
couple of local Idaho people – Fred and Rod. They had a
team of big clumping shire-horses which were pulling two
wagons in tandem. Initially there was a good deal of
unhealthy rivalry between the mule drivers and the new-
comers as each faction tried to prove the superiority of their
teams. Fred knew the area well and had offered to help with
working out routes and schedules. Jesse resented someone
new coming in and telling him how things should be run.
After all, he had got the wagon train this far. For a while the
wagon train became a bit of a race, with Jesse driving his
mules as hard as they could go while Fred's team of shires
followed up the rear. Fred and Rod thought that we ought
to take longer lunch stops and that we should travel a bit
more slowly.

A fundamental split was developing between the easterners and the westerners. Back east, wagon training is a huge
sport where over fifty thousand wagons hit the roads on
most summer weekends. The easterners favour light wagons
with rubber tyres and car seats. They are pulled by
fast-walking eastern-bred horses or mules. Western wagon

drivers take a more traditional approach and use heavy rigs with wooden wheels and hard bench seats. The wagons are pulled by big strong horses which walk more slowly but are able to pull much heavier loads. A western wagon train will aim to do a mere twelve to fifteen miles a day while the easterners like to crack on and do twenty or better. The difference is as much due to the traditions of horse breeding as to customs which go back as far as the civil war. The westerners dismiss the eastern wagons as being mere 'toys'. The easterners say that the traditionalists of the west only get their wagons out for parades and picnics.

The pioneer diaries make much of the rows and rivalries which developed on the wagon trains. The larger ones were always splitting up into smaller groups. Whole sections would break off and join other trains. One massive train of a hundred wagons set off along the trail in the 1850s. It finished with sixty wagons but only twelve of those had started out with the original group. Even with such a small wagon train as ours, there were fierce arguments over how fast or how slowly we should be travelling.

Some people make trouble, some make peace. Just when he was required, a teetotal Missouri farmer called Ralph Martin joined the wagon train. His arrival caused the disagreements to disappear just as fast as they had come. Ralph had loaded his team of mustang horses and his wagon on to a home-built trailer, hitched it up behind his truck and driven them the 1,500 miles from Missouri to join the wagon train. He was a God-fearing man with a laugh like a sewer rat and a line of dirty jokes which would be too crude for a miners' working club. No one could fail to take to him immediately.

A year earlier, his two mustangs had been running wild in the mountains of Colorado. They had been rounded up by government agents and sent to a special prison ranch where murderers, muggers and rapists are employed to 'halter-break' wild horses. This means holding on to a piece of rope attached to a head collar without getting dragged halfway across the state. These half-broken horses are then sold off for the knock-down price of 135 dollars apiece. Ralph had named his horses Yuma and Sante Fe after two of America's most notorious prisons.

Their arrival brought about a sudden change of atmosphere. Equilibrium was restored and the wagon train started working together. Jesse and Fred stopped trying to prove something to each other and both started trying to help Ralph with his half-wild and unfit team of horses.

Another key member of the wagon train was Harold Brown. He was always there at the back of the train with his orange flag. He had been a rural postman for thirty-five years and this was his retirement present to himself. He had kissed goodbye to his wife on the 1st of May and had not seen her since. He telephoned her once a week to say where he was so that she could put a pin in the map, and maybe another in Harold's effigy.

Harold had the horse which came closest to making the whole trail from start to finish. Ringo was nine years old – a cross between a Missouri foxtrotter and a Tennessee walker. He was a great horse who just set his head and walked out with a fluid gait. Ringo had only been off sick for one week, when a local rancher had loaned Harold a horse and then brought Ringo up to the wagon train in his trailer – a 250-mile round trip.

By the time I joined the wagon train in July Ringo already had a tired look in his eye. At night he would stand in the corral with his head hung low. Most horses will take a few mouthfuls of grass or hay and then lift their heads to take a look around. Ringo just kept his head down and continued munching with his eyes closed. Of all the animals on the wagon train Ringo was the one who most needed to spend three months under a tree and knee-deep in green grass.

Physically, Harold was not in much better condition than

his horse. He had been under the surgeon's knife three weeks before the wagon train departed and his doctor had advised him against taking the trip. But Harold had been planning on doing the Oregon Trail for the past five years and the good doctor realised that Harold had his heart set on going – whether or not his real heart was up to making the trip.

Harold's health fluctuated alarmingly. When he had had a bad night he would look as grey as an Edinburgh morning. He would crawl up on to Ringo's back and spend the day leaning heavily on his saddle horn. But Mr Brown had a spirit that could move mountains and by mid-day his mind had reasserted control of his ailing body and he was back to his cheerful self. To drop back and spend a few hours riding beside Harold was always a pleasure. He had any number of stories to tell – most were of doubtful veracity.

One day Mrs Brown went to see the doctor because she was pregnant. The doctor told her that she really should not be chewing tobacco while she was in her current state. She denied that she was a tobacco chewer. The doctor insisted that she was and that she had better pack it in – for the sake of the baby. The next time she went to see the doctor he said that he knew she was still chewing tobacco. He was greatly disappointed in her and again he warned her that she was risking the life of her unborn child.

It turned out that it was the doctor's wife who had told him about Mrs Brown and her disgusting habit. The doctor's wife had heard about it from the mechanic's wife. The mechanic had seen gobs of tobacco juice down the passenger door of Harold's car. However, he had forgotten that Harold worked for the post office and that rural postmen drive their cars sitting in the passenger seat with one hand on the wheel and their left foot operating the brake and accelerator. That way they can lean out of the passenger window and reach the mail boxes without getting out of the car. It was Harold who had been spitting tobacco juice out of the passenger window – and not making a very good job of it either.

We passed out of the irrigated potato land and into an area of wheat. The ground was bright yellow stubble as far as the eye could see. As I rode along with Harold at the back our train of conversation would be broken by a shout from one of the wagons as someone laid claim to an object spotted along the side of the road. The unwritten rules of wagon train etiquette dictate that he who spots something owns it. Both Jesse and Ralph had formidable collections of hub caps, mud flaps and car tax plates in their wagons. They had even more road junk in their barns. Spanners, screwdrivers and lumps of rope were common. Pitch forks – without handles, or without prongs, sometimes without either – were also picked up. Prize for the most useless article to have been spotted at the side of the road and carried along the trail was half a pair of scissors, which waited under Jesse's wagon seat for a matching half to be spotted. Even Jesse admitted that it was a long shot – but what a story he would have if he found it.

I suggested to Harold that the pickings must be pretty thin when riding flag on a big wagon train of thirty or more teams. He said that he had once picked up a pair of binoculars when riding flag on a train of fifty wagons with two hundred outriders.

Harold told me that at one time he and a friend had a rodeo clowning act which they used to tout around the amateur circuit. In one routine, Harold would pretend to be drunk and stagger into the ring with a big cardboard box bearing the name of a well-known brewer on the side. He would drop the box and a yellow liquid would come pouring out of the bottom. His partner would rush up with a jug to catch the amber nectar. He would drink it right down without offering Harold a single drop. The partner would rub his stomach and proclaim himself to be well pleased with his unexpected swig of beer. Harold would put down the box, open it up and out would come a cat.

I asked Harold if it was a real cat.

'Yup,' he said.

'Whose?'

'Just some local mog. We just grabbed the first one we could find as we came into town,' said Harold with a smile. I asked if people did not consider the act to be rather cruel on the cat. Harold reminded me that this was the best part of thirty years ago. 'Things were different then.' It is hard to apply a British measuring stick to the actions of people in another country with a different culture. To condemn Harold for his rodeo act would be as pointless as condemning an old age pensioner for keeping a budgie cooped up in a cage.

When the roads were quiet, Harold would occupy himself by singing hymns in an unbelievably flat base. He would stretch every consonant to its limit. He also wrote poetry – with a sting in the tail. He would deliver his verse in his quiet voice, the verses picking up the rhythm of Ringo's easy gait. My favourite was called 'The first time':

> The sky was blue, the moon was high,
> We were alone, just she and I,
> Her hair was brown, her eyes were too,
> She knew exactly what to do.
> Her lips were full, her body fine,
> I ran my fingers down her spine,
> I trembled and shook, and felt her heart,
> Then slowly she spread her legs apart.
> I knew she was ready, but I did not know how.
> You know that was my first experience
> Of milking a cow.

I liked Harold.

17

Summer boogers, prisoners of war and death on the road

My mother has always been particularly strong on picking noses. She regards it as a disgusting thing to do – possibly second only to having sex by yourself in her list of sins against self and humanity. In her book, a good blow into a clean, freshly ironed handkerchief is the only acceptable way of clearing out your nose.

Something new and terrifying was starting to happen to me. Each night I would find an incredibly hard lump of material stuck firmly in my nose. It would sit there, clinging like a limpet to my nasal hairs. I tried again and again to do it mother's way with the handkerchief and a good blow. They were resolute and refused to shift. I was beginning to wonder if something in my physiology had changed in some way. I found that my night-time routine came to include a guilt-ridden nose-picking session – carried out in the privacy of my tent. My private humiliation continued for some weeks until I overheard two of my travelling companions talking about 'summer boogers' and the dust in the air.

That single overheard conversation was like a weight off my mind. Suddenly I realised that rock-hard bogeys afflicted everyone who lived in these hot, dry and dusty conditions. The thought that Laurence of Arabia and even Princess Anne on her Save the Children expeditions must have spent many hours bogey picking made me feel a lot better about the world. I was beginning to wonder how much of surface of the gravel roads we were using was actually made of rock.

The air in Idaho was so dry that the sweat dried on the horses as quickly as it formed. The only way of telling that a horse was working hard was by a salty deposit that developed on its hair. This showed up fine on Ralph's black mustangs or on Fred's black shires but Roland had a lot of white hairs in his coat. I could only tell how hard he was working by monitoring the amount of water he drank. I watched his ears to count the number of mouthfuls of water. When the horses were working really hard their coats felt slightly granular with all the salt which had built up on them.

Most of the people on the wagon train were from wet parts of the USA – Tennessee, Missouri and Illinois all have decent rainfall. We were all amazed by the amount of irrigation and the human endeavour which went into getting water in Idaho to where it would do most good. The irrigated land on one side of the fence could be producing twenty tons of potatoes an acre while the unirrigated cattle pasture on the other side of the fence might be so poor that forty acres are needed to keep one thin cow alive (in Britain we have one cow on each acre of land).

We were following the Snake river right the way through Idaho. It has cut itself an incredibly deep canyon. To get the water to the flat land above the river valley required someone to start digging a canal forty or fifty miles back upstream. The canal had to be carefully brought along the edge of the valley and to have a gentle fall on it to keep the water flowing. Once it got to the lip of the valley thousands of miles of smaller irrigation canals could spread out like fingers and tendrils across the land.

And who did the digging? The Chinese – brought to the USA in their thousands and then sent back to their homeland once their job was done. And who does the

back-breaking job of moving the irrigation pipes and harvesting the onions and potatoes? The Mexicans – brought
to the USA as cheap labour and then sent back to their
homeland during the winter when their labour is no longer
required. We Europeans are not alone as exploiters.

The scenery changed rapidly depending on the presence
or absence of water. Sage brush desert one hour, then into
dry-land wheat with its thousand different shades of yellow
and brown, then into lush green fields of potatoes or
sweetcorn. It felt as though we were working our way
through a giant chequer board.

I began to enjoy the sage brush desert. The dirt roads
would pass through cattle grids and then scythe straight
across pastures which measured eight, ten or twelve thousand acres each. I could take off away from the wagon train
for an hour or more and just enjoy the riding, unencum-
bered by saddle bags or pack-horse. Both horses were
fantastically fit and they were on good feed. Rocky was a
real joy to ride. He was ridiculously sure-footed through
the scrub and over the gullies: I could canter him through
scrubland riddled with rabbit holes and surface roots and he
never missed a foot. And he was beautifully responsive to
the rein. In Britain we 'plough' rein our horses around by
pulling their heads to one side or another. This means that
you need to keep both hands on the reins. American horses
are trained to respond to the pressure of the rein on their
necks. The reins are held lightly in one hand and just by
moving your fist to left or right the horse feels the rein on
his neck and changes direction.

There is nothing to match the feeling of riding a responsive horse. You feel part of a single unit, sweeping across
country like a supercharged athlete. If Rocky spotted some
cattle he would start to tense, preparing himself for work,
and I wished that I could have tried him out as a cow pony.

Roland was different altogether. He still had his slow
walk so that when travelling with the wagon train I had to

trot for most of the day. But Roland travelled much better in the next gear up. He had a smooth mile-eating lope and if I could find a suitable bit of territory I could point him in the right direction and he would just settle into a smooth ground-covering stride. He was great as long as the ground was level but absolutely lousy over rough country. He came close to dumping me several times when I took off on some of my own little detours.

The evenings in the desert were wonderful. The temperature fell quite fast once the sun had gone down and the skies were the clearest I have ever seen: the dry air allows the starlight to shine through, undimmed by glows from city lights or pollution. Sometimes the coyotes would start their bizarre howling as they shouted their messages from hill to hill. There were some great talkers on the wagon train too.

Rod Mackay, the man who joined the train with Fred and the Clydesdales, walked with a bad limp. He had been a prisoner of war in Japan for three years. 'Stoops' he called the Japanese as an abbreviation of stupid. He had been captured in the Philippines in the early days of the war and been shipped back to Japan, 'lying like slaves' in racks on the boats. They were given one cup of water a day and one little bag of crackers on the trip. It was a whole month after he landed before he had a bowel movement. Rod watched many of his colleagues die on the ship and when his convoy was attacked by American submarines one of the ships went to the bottom with its cargo of American prisoners.

Once in Japan, Rod was sent to work on the docks, where the rations for each group of twenty servicemen were a bucket of rice and another of watery vegetable soup – about five hundred calories per man per day. Towards the end of the war an American bombing raid on the docks left only twenty-two of the fifty-five men in Rod's barrack house still alive. He said that they stood on the dockside the following night and cheered the planes which came over.

'None of us expected to survive. We thought the Stoops would kill us before we were liberated even if we survived the bombing raids.'

Rod put his bad knees and bad kidney down to mistreatment by the Japanese. I asked him what he thought of them today. He told me that he would never buy a Japanese car or television and that if he saw a lone Japanese tourist in the desert and thought he could get away with it, he would kill him. I looked into his face. He was very serious. Forgiving must be hard to do if you have suffered fifty years of pain in your legs and you need another plastic knee-cap which you cannot afford.

He recalled that the American liberation ships had expected to pick up thousands of American prisoners. Rod found himself one of a couple of dozen men on a hospital ship designed for thousands. 'We were outnumbered twenty to one by the nurses,' he said. The smile re-established its place on his face.

The next day we had to take the wagon train along a section of Highway 30 running through a town called Filer. It was a two-way road with hard shoulder on both sides. The wagon train was travelling west along the hard shoulder. I was talking to Fred and Rod when there was an immense crashing noise as two cars smashed into each other. All four teams started to run. Jesse was in front and managed to bring his three mules under control, and that brought the others to a halt behind him. Rocky's unflappability meant that he did little more than swing around to see where the danger was coming from.

There in the middle of the road was a badly smashed up American gas-guzzler. At first I could not see any other vehicle, then I noticed the side of a second car just sticking up from a dip at the side of the road. I tied Rocky to a fence and started running towards the car. A passing motorist had stopped and was leaning down through the upended car's window. I arrived just in time for him to pass an extremely bloody child into my arms. She was still strapped into her child's car seat. She was about two years old and was sobbing quietly. I carried her away from the car in case it caught fire and did my best to coo at her. I noticed that, despite the blood, she was still able to move both arms and legs. I did my best to keep her still. After what seemed like ages, a lady came up and took over from me. The car had been pushed back on to its wheels. Behind the wheel was a woman's face. The crimson blood on her cheek and forehead contrasted with the deathly grey of her skin. I noticed that the car was a small Japanese estate. It had California license plates. The driver of the American-built car was able to walk away from the crash.

A trucker had stopped and brought over an oxygen bottle. A number of other men were attending to the trapped woman as best they could. Someone said that the emergency services had already been called. I can remember the sound of the child's crying and the strained voices of the men who were trying to keep the unconscious woman alive. Ray was sitting in the back seat holding her head as she was given oxygen. I am told that the emergency services were on the scene within eight minutes – it felt like eight hours. They made Ray stay where he was, holding on to her and whispering into her ear while the medics cut her free. She was still alive but her body was bent in all the wrong places as they loaded her on to the stretcher. She looked as though she were about the same age as my wife, the child was the same age as my son. I imagined the woman turning around in the car to point out to the child such an exciting thing as a wagon train.

When they finally took the woman and the child away, Ray and I walked over to the fence where we had tied our horses. I leaned my head against Rocky's impassive flank. I looked up at Ray. He tried to hide the tears in his eyes – until he saw mine. We clasped hands across Rocky's back.

His were spattered with the lady's blood. Not a word passed between us.

That evening we heard on the news bulletins that the little girl was fine and would be discharged within a couple of days. The woman had died four hours after the accident. She was thirty-four years old – and was the child's grandmother.

We had flagmen out front and rear, we had taken every possible precaution, but we all knew that had we not been on the road with our horses, flags and wagons then that lady would still be alive.

She was driving a Japanese car. Rod blamed 'them damn Stoops'.

18

Sherlock Holmes, Jesus on the radio and working goldfish

It is hard to describe the noise made by coyotes. They howl, they yip, they wail. They make noises which sound like nothing else on earth. Their incomprehensible messages pass through the countryside from pack to pack. It is impossible to know how far these waves of communication have come or what they mean. To be lying in my sleeping bag, listening to Derek Nimmo on the BBC World Service attempting to stutter his way through a one-minute monologue on potatoes, while the natural coyote cacophony surged around me, was an extreme form of weirdness. The radio plays which frequently appear on the BBC World Service were also extremely hard to keep tabs on because the characters kept dropping out of earshot along with the short wave signal. People who had been introduced to the plot while the signal was having a holiday would suddenly appear. Sherlock Holmes would have been hard pressed to make sense of it.

However, American radio can offer plenty of madness. As we approached Boise, the largest town in Idaho, the wavelengths started to fill. One evening I picked up a station which was broadcasting a soap opera. It seemed to involve a young woman getting up to go to work. The alarm clock rang and she turned it off. She did not want to get up but she put her feet on to the cold floor, threw on a dressing-gown and put the kettle on for coffee. She was late for work again. Just as she was leaving the house the phone rang. It was a voice she knew well.

'Hello Jesus,' she said. 'How are you today?'

'Very well,' said Jesus. 'But more to the point, how are you? Can I come to work with you today?'

As Mary walked out of the apartment door Jesus was there to greet her. They sat on the bus and chatted on the way to work. Jesus hung up her coat for her and Mary put a chair beside her desk for Jesus to sit on. Not once during the soap opera did any of Mary's work colleagues notice anything odd about Mary – not even the fact that her coat hung itself on the hook every morning when she got to work.

I had been listening to several religious stations during my journey. For the American entrepreneur, running a religious radio station seemed to be no different from running any other – country, rock, religious. They pump out a diet of religious soap operas and Christian songs. The stations can also rent their signal to the radio equivalent of pyramid selling. The air-time will be devoted to a one-hour show, often a phone-in, where people can call in for Christian counselling. Many claim to be the victims of satanism – young girls and boys mostly – who give lurid descriptions of their tribulations. The host of these pro-grammes is able to switch seamlessly between a compassion-ate soft voice, which is used for addressing the callers, and a hectoring pulpit-style oratory which is used to appeal to the listeners for money.

'I started this programme with an appeal for four saints to step forward with a thousand dollars each. I have heard from not one. Not one Christian saint. Will not one of you out there help this poor girl, victim of the works of the devil? This poor woman needs help, she needs Christian help which only we can give. But we need your help, your credit card number.'

The money given is used to buy more air-time on more

stations so that more money can be donated so that more air-time can be bought.

I am not sure that God would entirely approve of some of the radio stations which broadcast in His name.

One evening the wagon train pulled up at a cattle corral which was pretty close to nowhere but forty miles from Boise. The ranch manager was a laconic cowboy called Wayne. He was half Mexican, half Finnish, but all American. He agreed I could come along when he went out and rode some of his pastures that evening but said that he would prefer me to ride one of his horses. We set off in his truck with two cow ponies in the back. When they were unloaded they turned out to be long lanky animals – more English thoroughbred than stumpy quarter horse. Wayne confirmed that on this thin scrubland the cattle were few and far between and that he needed horses which could cover the miles. A real cowboy spends most of his time riding around the countryside looking for sick cattle. Any he finds are roped and treated – usually with a huge shot of antibiotics.

About fifteen minutes into the ride my horse started bucking. I was rather surprised. Up until then he had been fine. The cowboys at the Nebraska rodeo had raised one hand high in the air and 'grabbed sky' when riding a bucking horse. I 'grabbed saddle' and clung on tight while this skinny brute of a horse tried to get me off its back. I managed to stay more or less seated and the horse stopped bucking just as quickly as it had started.

Wayne rode up to me with a smile on his face and said, 'Sorry. Clean forgot he does that sometimes.' I think I had passed the test.

Wayne was quietly proud of his job, especially the fact that he never drove a tractor. When I mentioned that to call someone a cowboy in England was an insult, he was about as horrified as his laconic character would allow him to be.

He asked me when I would be getting home to my wife and family. I had been asked the question so many times that I had a standard answer.

'I should get to sleep with my own wife and ride my own horse some time in the beginning of October,' I said.

Wayne rode on in silence for a moment, then said, 'Round here we usually do things the other way about.' It would have been nice to have had time to get to know him – a couple of decades should have been enough.

When we turned up that evening there was no water in the corral where I had left Rocky and Roland. The surrounding pasture was typical sage scrub with a narrow strip of green where the stream-bed ran through. The gully was completely dry, although moisture must be present because there were even a few willows amongst the other trees along the stream. I dug a hole to see if I could get to the moisture but got down two feet without finding any.

There was water in the pasture but it was three hundred yards away in a dew-pond down the hill. I walked the horses down there to give them a drink and was amazed to find that it was full of goldfish. To see their bright golden bodies flickering in this muddy scraping seemed incongruous. Ray told me that they often put goldfish in ponds and even in drinking troughs. The fish keep the weed down and also give the ranchers an instant indication that the water is fit for the stock to drink.

Rocky and Roland only had halters on but I did not feel like walking back so I jumped up on to Rocky's back and started to walk them back towards the corral. I was feeling quite pleased with myself for having passed Wayne's little riding test so I urged Rocky into a canter. Betty saw us come up the brow of the hill and asked if I would go back and do it again while she ran her video camera.

I turned Rocky back towards the pond and as I did so Ralph threw a bucket at his legs. Rocky leapt sideways but I held on. I took the horses back to the pond and then cantered them back up towards the camp site. Rocky started to run a bit faster but I let him open up for the sake of the pictures. As I approached the wagons, I noticed that Ray and Ralph had armed themselves with buckets and were preparing to pelt us. I asked Rocky for a sudden change of direction, he gave it to me, and we started to circle away from the wagons. Rocky thought this was a good game, so his head came up and he went up a gear or three. Since he only had a halter on, I really had no control of him at all. I let go of Roland's lead rope to concentrate on staying aboard. Rocky swung in towards the corral where his feed was and started heading for the gate – which was closed.

I was confident that Rocky would be able to stop before he hit the gate but I was not optimistic that I would stop with him. I decided to bail out. Well, that is my story anyway.

I landed hard on my right elbow and hip. Actually, when you pass thirty-five all landings are hard ones. Ray was the first to get to me as I lay on the ground. I could see a look of genuine compassion in his eyes as he helped me to get up. He was the sort of person who pretended to be a hard man but every now and then the barrier would come down. It was the second time in a week that he had let me see the real Ray rather than the hard truck driver or trail boss. The hip would later develop a magnificent blue and yellow bruise and my elbow and forearm were badly grazed by hitting the dirt at twenty miles an hour. Gene, who also came up to see how I was after my fall, noticed the cuts on my forearm and went off to get some ointment. He squirted a dollop of it into my hand, telling me that it would make it better and take the pain away. It made the cuts sting like hell. I took the bottle off him and saw that it was horse liniment. He laughed. I would have washed the stuff off, except I thought that the stagnant pond would be full of unpleasant bacteria. That night I slept on my left side but the stinging in the arm kept me awake.

The next morning I went over to inspect the hole I had dug in the stream-bed. The stream was flowing even though there had been no rain. Wayne came over to see us off and told me that the stream was fed by a spring half a mile back up the hill. It slowly dries up during the heat of the day as the plants along the bed greedily suck it dry. At night the temperature falls and the plants at the top give those further down a chance to get some moisture.

Two days later we paraded right through the centre of Boise – the state capital of Idaho and the biggest town on the Oregon Trail. It seemed immense and disgustingly busy compared to the open country we had been travelling through for the previous week or two. We were met on the edge of town by the local drill team called the Posse-ettes. They escorted us right through the city centre and to the state capital where that nice Mr Cecil Andrews of the Guberif met us. On the way we passed a car dealer called Fairly Reliable Bob's. It was a massive place. I imagined trying to start a business in Britain with such a name. The high street banks would not regard it as a good risk.

'Fairly Reliable Bob's . . . No, Mr Winter, I think something more respectable such as Clutterbuck and Davies might be more suitable, don't you?'

We also passed a showroom run by a man who billed himself as 'Dave Mockowitz, the Singing Car Dealer'. Then there was a shop called 'Idaho hub caps'. The man was standing outside his shop watching us go past. I had to ask. He sold nothing but hubcaps. He had 25,000 of them in stock and said he could easily supply ones which would fit Jesse's wagon. Only in America. I hope.

19

Thunder eggs, farrier baiting and fishing with dynamite

Crossing into Oregon was a great day for all of us. Rocky and I had been on flag duty at the front of the wagon train. The road was busy with traffic but to make things worse it undulated as it headed west. The truck drivers needed to keep their speed high to get them over the roller-coaster of short hills and dips. Suddenly a cloud of black smoke would appear over the brow of a hill. Within seconds the tip of a chromed smoke stack would appear. Then came the thundering monster of a truck – shining, noisy and menacing. Rocky and I had to canter ahead to the brow of each hill to wave the flag at the oncoming traffic. Then as the wagon train came into sight we had to move on ahead to the crest of the next hill along. It was hot, sweaty and stressful work – although Rocky seemed to relish the change in routine.

Most drivers slowed down as soon as they saw us. Others ignored the bizarre site of a man on a horse in the middle of the road waving a fluorescent orange flag at them. Only when they actually saw the wagon train for themselves would they suddenly slam on their brakes with a huge hiss. Rocky would have made a good police horse. I would have felt distinctly nervous had I been riding Roland.

As the wagon train crossed the bridge over the Snake and entered Oregon we felt as though we were on the home straight – although we were still nearly a month away from the end of the trail. Our first night in the new state was spent at a place called Nyssa – 'Thunder egg capital of the world'. Thunder eggs are nodules of rock formed in the heat of volcanoes, the size of nobbly grapefruit. They can be cut in half to reveal a series of concentric rings of crystal. Every now and then a hollow one turns up. Then it is full of tiny stalagmites and stalactites like a glittering high rise city.

We spent the night at the Nyssa rodeo grounds and it was here that I offended Jesse for the second time. I had been extremely careful to avoid a repeat of the alcohol incident back at Cokeville when I first met the wagon train.

I had with me a large pillow-sized water container. When we pulled into camp at night I would fill the water container and set it in the sun. By dusk I would have a couple of gallons of hot water available for a shower. I would go off to find a tree to hang the container in, strip off and turn on the tap. It was wonderful.

There were no trees at the Nyssa rodeo ground and the best place I could find was a hook on the underside of the commentary box. I thought I was well out of sight of the wagon train and it was nearly dark anyway. I was standing there in the altogether, nice and soapy, when I caught sight of Jesse. He said something to me which I did not catch. I assumed that he must have made some sort of joke so I laughed.

Clean, tidy and feeling pretty good, I went over to join my fellow travellers. It took me a while before I noticed a distinct chill in the atmosphere. It was coming from Jesse. Yet again it fell to Ray to take me aside and explain that Jesse was extremely upset about my behaviour. He was concerned that one of the womenfolk might have stumbled upon me 'naked as a jay bird'. He also said that I could have been seen from the houses on the edge of town.

I said rather flippantly that if anyone could see anything from the houses one of us had something to be proud of, they of their night vision or me of my manhood. Perhaps a bit more remorse might have been appropriate.

The next morning I went over to the toilet block for my constitutional. The toilets at Nyssa are of a unique design. There is one big room with half a dozen conventional toilet stalls, each of a different design, colour and style; there are no partitions at all. It looks more like a toilet museum than a functioning convenience. The door had been pushed closed so I shouted out to see if anyone was in occupation.

Jesse told me to come right on in. I expected to see him having a wash at the sink but he was sitting down with his overalls around his ankles. To have turned around and left him to it might have caused offence. Besides, 'a man's got to do what a man's got to do'. In this case Jesse clearly did not think it necessary to do it alone. So I took down my trousers and sat down beside him. We had a wide-ranging chat about mules, wagon trains and deserts. I thought he might raise the subject of showers and nakedness but he let it lie. And so did I.

Eastern Oregon proved to be drier than I had expected. Oregon has the image of being green, covered in timber and inhabited by lumberjacks. Most of the state is as dry as Idaho and Wyoming. The emigrants must have been getting very disappointed by the time they got this far. They had been on the road for four or five months and still they were in dry hot land, totally at odds with the sort of country described in the guide books.

I was having a great time. The trip had turned into something of a holiday now that I did not have to worry about routes and overnight stops. And now that the pressure was off, Rocky and Roland also became easier to manage. They were thriving on their one day on, one day off routine. Twenty-five miles every day is bad for a horse, twenty-five miles every other day is good for them.

The mules were doing extremely well and were proving themselves to be equal to the physical challenges of the trip. They had lost all their hair where the harness rubbed against their skin but they were not at all sore. It was a fine sight to see Joe, Sandine and Bull, Jesse's three mules, leaning into their collars as they hauled the wagon. Their long ears flopped back and forth, twice for every stride – twelve million ear flops along the length of the trail. They mouthed their bits as they walked and Joe always had his tongue hanging way out to one side of his mouth. Sandine, who had the nicest temperament of all the mules on the wagon train, liked to be stroked and was safe to be around. I even rode him for a while one day – he was extremely uncomfortable. I started to think seriously about getting my own mare at home in England in foal to a donkey. I rather fancied the idea of riding around the lanes of Buckinghamshire on a mule.

Kate and Allie on the other wagon were also doing well, although Allie was as hard as ever to shoe. No one on the wagon train would touch her. When she needed doing Harold or Paula would get on the phone to find a farrier who was prepared to have a go. The poor man would come over to camp and we would all gather around to watch the sport. I wondered if there was some insurance company which specialised in injury claims for farriers: it would be able to trace our progress across America by a chain of injured farriers. Allie had to be roped up to stop her lashing out with deadly accuracy but then she would lean right down on the unfortunate farrier. Pride usually ensured that he saw the job through to its end. Watching Allie's attempts to maim the farrier I had second thoughts about getting Molly in foal to a donkey.

The horses were less robust than the mules. One of Ray's horses got badly injured on a roadside crash barrier and spent a week off work before it was decided that he needed a much longer rest. He was left behind in Baker City; Ray was going to pick him up on the way home.

One of Ralph's mustangs started to develop respiratory problems. Strangely enough it was his right hand one – just as the pioneers' right-hand animals had suffered from being forced to walk in the dust generated by their partners. We put Roland in harness and he did his turn pulling the wagon. I spent the day learning to drive a team while Ralph recounted an endless stream of dirty jokes. As far as I could tell he never repeated any but I understood only about a third of them. Some were lost in the cultural gap between us, others disappeared behind his strong Missouri accent. But Ralph laughed so hard at his own jokes that he never seemed to notice whether anyone else joined in. I never found out where he got all the jokes from, as he never drank and assured me that his social life revolved around the church.

The targets of his humour were Texans, women, blacks, Texans, Indians and homosexuals. It seems that Texans are to America what Yorkshiremen are to Britain. Both have that quiet, understated pride in the knowledge that they are the finest people on earth because they were born in the finest place on earth. It ensures their universal popularity.

'How do you tell a Texan? You can't tell him anything,' was just one of many in Ralph's repertoire. His favourite joke was to take his cowboy boots off and place them on the bench beside him. He would then place his hat on top of the boots and ask 'What's that?'

'A Texan with the shit kicked out of him' was the reply.

Ralph had a little American flag which he would wave at passing motorists. If he saw someone in their garden he would wave his flag and shout, 'Get your horse, saddle up and come with us.' If he saw someone with a dog he would always offer to buy it, saying that we needed a good guard dog.

Then there was Betty. She was the person who had actually started the wagon train rolling. She always claimed that she never wanted to organise a wagon train in the first place. Her plan was simply to follow along with her video camera, make a film and sell it. She had worked out that if

everything went right she would end up with over thirty
thousand dollars. However, as the winter months ticked
past she realised that no one else was going to write all the
necessary letters, so she sat down at her kitchen table and
made a start. First to the newspapers asking for people to
help and act as guides through each area. The response was
extremely patchy. In some areas locals took on the whole
job. They worked out the route, organised places for us to
stay and laid on food for us and the animals. At other times
we were completely by ourselves and did not really know
from one night to the next where we might be able to stay.
Betty told me that the Nebraskans were brilliant, the
Wyomings (what is the collective term for people who live
in Wyoming?) were almost non-existent, the Idahoans
were better than brilliant and the Oregonians were fine –
but spread pretty thin across their state.

By any measuring stick, Betty was a remarkable woman. I
asked her if she was having a good time on the wagon train,
adding that I would be surprised if she was. She had realised
that her plans were not working out and she was going to
lose a large amount of money on this venture. She said
that she was having an 'experience'. And the high spot? – a
journalist's question if ever there was one.

Betty said that one incident she would never forget was
when she was propositioned by an eighty-year-old farmer.
He had replied to one of her pleas for help in a local paper,
offering a place for the wagon train to stay. He turned up
the night before to introduce himself and declared his
excitement at seeing the wagon train. The next day he
turned up and took Betty off to get some good distance
shots with her video camera. When she finished her filming
and climbed back into his truck, he did not start his engine
but leaned across to place his hand on her knee. He turned
his watery-blue eyes on her and said, 'Betty, I want to tell
you that I am so excited to see you. You know, last night I
woke up with the biggest erection I have had in a decade.

That's not bad for an eighty-year-old man. I just wanted to share that with you, Betty.'

Betty started her life as a Catholic. She married a Catholic and started producing babies, like a good Catholic wife should. By the time she was twenty-five she had six children and an absentee husband. Every Sunday she dressed her kids as well as her budget allowed and took them off to church. She even paid her tithe. The priests decided that they needed two million dollars to build a wonderful new church. They asked for an extra tithe. Betty asked to be let off; she said it was a case of paying up or letting the kids go to school in bare feet. The priests suggested that she should pay the tithe first and then hope that God would find a way to put shoes on her children. Betty decided that this was not good enough. Her six kids were all under seven. In the eyes of the Catholic Church they were too young to have sinned and would be guaranteed a place in heaven – should they die. Betty suggested to the priests that the best thing she could do for them was to go home and murder them all.

She said that she was just trying to make a point. She certainly did that. The priests put a shrink on to her and Betty spent a lot of time convincing people that she did not intend to murder her kids.

After that Betty lost her faith in God but she got it back a few years later when she had a terrible road accident. She said she died three times on the operating table and each time she went to a wonderful place full of wonderful people. She wanted to stay but the wonderful people told her to go back to earth. It was not time to leave yet.

I asked her about her relationship with God. She quoted President Reagan at me. Apparently, once over dinner, Reagan was asked whether he believed in God. He said that he really liked the meal he was eating and added, 'It is hard to believe that this came together without a cook.'

'I am not saying God is benevolent though,' said Betty. 'He has a terrible mean streak. Look at the marriage partners

He fixes most people up with. They think they are marrying one sort of person and find that they are shackled to something entirely different. God packs a grudge like you would not believe. He put temptation in front of Adam and Eve, then He got mad at them and threw them out of Eden. Now God punishes us for something we did not do and expects us to love Him for it. And what sort of person sends his son to earth and then stands by to let him be crucified?'

'And you are going to go to Heaven when you die?' I asked.

'I know I am,' she said.

Three days after entering Oregon we stayed at a little cluster of houses called Brogan. It used to have three banks, a proper school, its own branch line off the railway, three fruit-packing warehouses and a couple of hotels. Now there is a café – which is up for sale – and half a dozen houses. The people of Brogan gave us a wonderful evening of entertainment.

I had always dismissed ghost towns as nothing more than a cliché created by the American movie industry. However, there are thousands of these sad places scattered all over the west. The whole idea of a town which has disappeared in living memory is alien to someone from Britain, where you can find places where towns once existed hundreds of years ago but not towns which have gone from boom to bust in the space of a decade or less.

That evening I got talking to a splendid old lady called Lola Reeves who had once been a schoolteacher at Brogan. Later on, we sneaked off to see her friend Alma Crawley, who lived in an old people's home in the nearby town of Ontario. Alma had kept all sorts of photographs and newspapers from the old town and what could have been an evening of sombre talk about the demise of a town turned out a cheerful affair as the two old ladies laughed their way through past history.

Brogan had been born out of a money-making scheme dreamed up by an easterner called Denis Brogan. He had noticed that the soil in the area was extremely fertile but terribly dry. The spot had a second major advantage in that it seldom suffered from bad frosts in the spring. If he could just get water to the land, it would be able to support fruit orchards. Denis Brogan did some surveying work and discovered that the building of an earth-bank reservoir and ten miles of canal could 'make the desert bloom' and convert land worth a mere two dollars an acre into land worth a hundred dollars an acre. Not having too much money of his own, he went back east, raised the money and in 1908 came back to Brogan and bought the land at rock-bottom prices.

Four years later, the twelve-year-old Alma Crawley had come to Brogan on the newly installed railway line, which the locals called Sage Brush Anny.

'My father had picked up a brochure about Brogan back home in Kansas. He had sold everything and come here to start a new life. It looked like it was nowhere,' said Alma. 'But my father had bought sixty acres of it.'

Lola Reeves had come to Brogan in 1918 to teach at the school. At ninety-three, she is still treated with school-teacher deference by her seventy-five-year-old former first-grade pupils. By 1918 there were two or three shops, a couple of hotels and the banks – and there were over 1,600 acres of orchards and some extremely fine farm land. Each forty-acre farm supported a family and one full-time worker. During the picking season the population of the town increased fourfold as migrant workers poured in to help gather the harvest. Those in the packing sheds were working around the clock to prepare fruit for the long journey back east. There was also a thriving dairy industry and a lot of vegetable land.

Lola and Alma laughed as they remembered how exciting it was to be young and highly marriageable women in a boom town brimming over with ambitious young men.

Lola showed me a picture of her as a young woman sitting on the roof of a railway box-car with her feet hanging over the side. There seemed to be quite a lot of leg on display for a picture taken in 1919. I asked her how she got up there. She told me that there was a ladder at one end. 'The boys helped me up,' she said as both she and Alma burst into peals of laughter. There did not seem to be any trace of resentment or sadness at what had slipped away from them.

Lola eventually chose to marry a farmer who came to Brogan from Iowa. He was called Axel and he managed his forty-acre patch of land with one hand. He had lost the other in an accident.

'How ?' I asked Lola.

'Fishing,' she said with a smile. She looked across at Alma. This was a familiar routine to them. I had been hooked and reeled right in. They knew that I had to ask how you could lose a hand fishing.

'He was fishing with dynamite,' said Lola and the two of them started to cackle all over again. Their hard lives had shaped a hard sense of humour.

The town grew and flourished, people kept on pouring in and the land prices rose and rose. Then in 1930 they had a dry year, and another in 1931, and again in 1932. The farmers watched as the water-level fell in the reservoir. They had some terrible town meetings when they decided that they would have to ration their water. That is a hard decision to make. An arable farmer can lose a whole crop and come back next year and try again. If fruit farmers lose their trees they have to wait another ten years before they can establish another crop. The families which had come to Oregon, land of hope, had to stand by and watch their precious trees wither away. The banks realised that it would be ten years, at best, before these farms came back into pro-duction, so they pulled out. The packing sheds closed, the railway went rusty. In the space of a couple of years the town folded in on itself. Those who remained moved over to a barter economy. People were afraid to put money in the bank in case the bank went bust.

By the middle of the 1930s the Malhuer Reservoir was as dry as a bone. The rain came back in the 1940s but by then it was too late to save the farmers. The reservoir ran dry again during the fifties. During the sixties, seventies and eighties it was full and became a popular water-skiing resort. Launch ramps, public toilets and camp sites were built all around its perimeter. Now they have all been abandoned. The reservoir is again dry.

20

Chinese miners, lost dreams and a murder in Texas

The next day I was up before the sun. I walked through the sage brush to take the buckets of grain over to Rocky and Roland. They whickered their happiness that breakfast had arrived. As they ate, I looked across the valley at Brogan, and at the hills in the distance. They are now covered in sage. Forty-acre holdings which once supported a whole family and a hired hand now support one measly range cow. The bottom land is down to dry-land crops. I tried to imagine Brogan when the town and the trees were in full bloom, with peach, apple and pear blossom spreading across the hills. I am not sure that I could have been as cheerful about the town's demise as Lola and Alma had been the previous evening.

We took the wagons across the flat valley floor and up into the Spring Creek Canyon where a small brook burbled its way along beside our dirt road. A whole community had pinned its prosperity and very existence on this tiny stream of water. Two eighteen-inch-wide strips of bright green grass followed the river but that was all. Within three foot-steps of the bank the soil reverted to dust. Sage was the only vegetation. On this land, merely being near to water is not enough to guarantee life, the water must be flowing right through it.

Spring Creek Canyon was deep, dark and cool. I put my sweatshirt back on as we entered its shady recesses. The floor of the valley was littered with neatly stacked piles of rocks, ten feet high and thirty feet across. They looked like the abandoned foundations of a great dry-stone city. One of the locals who was travelling with us explained that they were the remains of some of the old goldmine workings. Randy said that thousands of Chinese labourers had been brought in to dig up the canyon floor and wash out the dirt for the gold dust which lay here. The stones were the rocks which were too big to be placed in the washing channels. The claims were small and the stones had to be neatly stacked to avoid dumping them on the land belonging to the next group of miners.

This desolately empty place had once been alive with the noise and activity of people who had been transported thousands of miles from an alien culture to work here. Now it was peaceful and quiet save for the sound of hooves on gravel and the gentle jingle of harness. No one on the wagon train shouted or sang; we travelled in silence, over-come by the sight of so much work and effort and lost opportunities. In England we are used to the old being replaced by the new but the old being replaced by nothing at all, just dereliction, is something else again.

Then Randy pointed high up on the western side of the canyon wall. A dead straight line, incongruous against the natural forms of the rock, ran level and true. It hugged the canyon wall, fighting for height as it went. It was the old canal which had taken water from a diversion ten miles further up the canyon. It had picked the river up from the valley floor and contained it in a concrete and dry-stone channel, climbing the rocky canyon wall until it emerged halfway up a mountain above the water-hungry fields of Brogan.

The canal, all twelve miles of it, had been built by the Chinese brought to Malhuer County to provide the muscle power and skill needed to run the mine workings. The gold was running out at the time that Dennis Brogan came here to survey his nirvana and the Chinese labourers needed his money to pay for their passage home. Brogan's dream was built on the ashes of the mining industry of Malhuer County.

As we moved up the canyon, the sun was working its way down the eastern wall. Our route was made even darker by the brightness of the desert sunlight which was striking the rocks above our heads. The sun did not penetrate to the canyon floor until sometime after ten. Then the temperature started to rise. It kept on rising. Within an hour it was too hot for comfort and a bit of shade would have been nice. These were the mountains which, in the flowery prose of Alma's 1910 Brogan brochure, 'store the energy of the sun by day and release it by night'. I thought we were in danger of being cooked during the storing-up period. Those Chinese miners must have been tough to have carried on working in this sort of airless, stifling heat.

By lunchtime we had passed out of the valley and on to a large plateau which had once been the reservoir. Cattle were grazing the tussocky grass in the flat bottom land. Malhuer County was going through one of its occasional periods of drought. Five years ago the whole lot had been under water. Ski-boats would have been whizzing around twenty feet above the scrub where the cattle were now grazing. The ramps for launching boats led from one bit of sage brush and dirt down to another bit of sage brush and dirt. The camp sites were abandoned.

We stopped for lunch at an immaculate little cemetery. It had once been on the edge of a small mining town called Malhuer City with ten thousand miners living in the area. Brothels, smoking-dens, bars, churches and homes had been built – now they had all gone. The post office closed there in 1948, a sure sign that even the government had given up on the place. Now there is nothing to be seen but the remains of a couple of stone cellars and an awful lot of sage. Most of the houses were built of timber and would have been consumed in the frequent range fires which sweep this area. There is just one small white hut. Each spring, on Memorial Day, the surviving ex-inhabitants of Malhuer City meet for a meal there. Over the door, in neat black letters, is the legend, 'Malhuer City – Land of Lost Dreams'. We walked around the graveyard reading the names of the miners and their families – the people who had given their lives for a dream.

The travelling was a dusty business. It was getting to the horses as well as to us. Yuma, one of Ralph's mustangs, had never been right since he started to get ill back in Idaho. His nose was perpetually streaming and he was leaving his partner, Santa Fe, to do most of the work. Ralph had been borrowing one of Jesse's mules as well as Roland to help pull his wagon in order to give Yuma some rest days. However, we all recognised that a more permanent solution was required and we had put the word out to the locals that we needed another mule. The idea was that Ralph would be able to rotate the three animals so that they only had to work two days out of three.

Somehow or other Ralph managed to acquire a two-year-old mule called Buster. He was absolutely beautiful – a lovely glossy coat, bright eyes and tough little feet. The trouble was that he had never been ridden or asked to pull a wagon. Jesse and Ralph spent a couple of evenings working on him and within two days he was hitched to a wagon beside Sante Fe and he started his new career.

After three days in the dry dusty mountains we followed the Burnt River Canyon down towards Durkee. Six miles from the bottom we were met by twenty people on horses. They were two ranching families – three generations ranging from four years old to seventy. The men and their wives were riding the working quarter horses. Ponies are comparatively rare in the west and kids are given the old, retired ranch horses to ride. A four-year-old child sitting on the back of a full-size horse looks ridiculous. Their tiny legs come nowhere near the stirrups, they bounce along as they cling to the horn on an over-size western saddle, their tiny legs waving miles out of range of the stirrups. But their mounts have learned their trade from the best horsemen in the world. They know what signals a rider should give them. They have been trained to obey the correct instructions and follow them – no more, no less. They have been on the ranches for twenty or thirty years and are trusted members of the family. The kids learn to ride on these wonderful old retainers.

We do it all wrong in Europe. We put out kids on nasty little ponies which have been allowed to get away with bad habits like biting and kicking. Half the kids who ride in Britain are scared of their mounts – and the ponies know it. A ranch horse spends the first ten or twelve years of its life being ridden hard and well. They are working horses and bad habits would get in the way of productivity. There are few bad horses, and those are sold off down to the meat plant.

The families who came out to meet the wagon train escorted us to one of their best pastures. It was the first real grass we, or our stock, had seen for months. The grass was knee-deep and a beautiful natural green. There were full-size oak trees and a stream running through one end of the field. It was the sort of pasture you take entirely for granted in England. We closed the gate and turned the animals loose. They thought they had died and gone to heaven. They rolled and kicked their feet in the air, they thundered around like a gang of excited children. Even Harold's horse, Ringo, made an effort and joined in the general excitement. Then the horses and mules dropped their heads into the fine green grass and started to eat. Their tails flicked contentedly. The only sound was the occasional contented snort or fart.

That evening we had a barbecue under the trees. I noticed that several of my companions lay down on the cool grass and fingered it as we talked and yarned with the ranchers. It was not just the horses who had been missing the green. Every now and again the horses and mules would come galloping and kicking past as they celebrated their full bellies and good fortune.

I pitched my tent and the turf felt like a feather mattress after the unyielding dirt of the desert. I woke up in the night with a start. I had rolled over on to my right side and bashed my grazed arm. It made me think of Gene and the horse liniment he had given me to put on. He must have known that it would sting. I lay there, listening to the sound of the animals grazing close by the tent. In the distance the coyotes were howling in the Malhuer Mountains we had just left behind. Of all the people on the wagon train, Gene in his western clothes was the most 'authentic'. He always had a long Bowie knife in a scabbard on the back of his belt. He had a six-gun in the glove box of his truck and I am reasonably sure that there was one in the blanket roll he always had across the back of his saddle. He was almost never without his hat – even on the few occasions when we went indoors. Without it, his bald head and grey hair made him look every one of his sixty years; with it on, he could have been taken for a man of forty.

When we made camp, Gene would always park his rig a discreet distance from everyone else. He would often sit alone in the evenings, or he would spend hours talking and petting his horses. When we were travelling across open range land he would take big swings out into the country-side, often leaving the wagon train for hours at a time. He could sometimes be glimpsed sitting on his horse up away on a distant hill. An hour later he and his horse Ruby might come trotting up the road to rejoin the wagon train or we might come around a bend in the road to find him sitting under a tree waiting for us while Ruby grazed at the verge. He and his wife of three months had joined the trip back in Nebraska but by the time I joined, in Idaho, he was travelling alone. Judy was his sixth wife. While still with the wagon train it emerged that her previous marriage had not been properly annulled. Technically she was a bigamist. Gene bought her a pick-up truck and told her to go away. She did. Two months later Judy reappeared. She had sorted out the paperwork and the two of them were back together again.

Back home in Colorado Gene had a ranch where he bred horses and dogs. The dogs were a cross of his own invention, made between a wolf and a Rottweiler. He assured me that they 'could' make safe family pets.

I asked my fellow travellers what they knew about Gene. 'Not all that much' was the answer. Ray told me a tale about how he and Jesse had been looking for rattlesnakes while the wagon train was stopped for lunch. They were trying to grab hold of one angry snake using a set of rattler sticks. These are three-foot-long steel tubes with a pair of strong steel fingers on the end which can be opened and closed with a lever let into the handle. They are like the tongs old-fashioned grocers used to use to get cereal packets down off high shelves. By all accounts, Ray and Jesse had made rather a hash of catching this particular rattlesnake and things were getting rather messy. The snake had escaped the sticks and was heading for the two men – an unusual thing for a snake to do and they both felt as though they were on a bit of a sticky wicket – although that is not how they would have described their predicament. Suddenly, they saw a flash of steel as a knife whizzed passed Jesse's shoulder. The tip of the blade went right through the snake's neck and into the ground. The snake was very nearly decapitated there and then. It was certainly dead, although its nervous system had not quite got the message yet. Gene was standing some twenty feet back with a quiet smile on his face.

'I thought you needed some help,' he said.

As the days became weeks I got to know Gene better – not that anyone could get to know him well. He had two horses, a small Appaloosa called Kid, as tough and strong an animal as you could wish for, but he was over ten years old and starting to suffer from rheumatism. When the travelling was hard he needed dosing up with pain-killers to keep him going. Gene had another, much bigger horse, a mare called Ruby. She was strong but only three years old and a comparative baby. Ruby walked almost as slowly as Roland. We once had a ten-dollar bet to see whose horse could walk the slowest without actually stopping. Ruby won. Just.

It suited Gene and I to ride along together. We would let our slow-coach horses amble along for a few miles as we dropped further and further behind the wagon train. Then we would trot or lope for a while and close the gap. We did not talk a lot but we usually had a rather strung-out conversation going for most of the time. He would say something, then I would say something. Nothing more might be added for half an hour or more until one of us dropped another sentence into the pot. It might take us a whole day to exchange as many words as most people might burn up in ten minutes.

We often talked about horses. On this particular subject the flow of information was generally one-way. I had a lot to learn, he had a lot to teach. But some days the scope of the conversation widened. He had seen military service in Korea, where he was in one of the snatch squads sent behind enemy lines to rescue prisoners of war.

'Those guys,' he told me one day when he seemed more talkative than usual, 'were in a terrible state when we picked them up – those that were still alive that is. Laid down their weapons and surrendered in good faith. They were rewarded by being treated like animals. Worse than animals. I vowed then that no one would ever take away my weapon or lock a door on me.'

Gene said that he preferred horses to people because they never lie to you. They will not be telling you one thing while slipping the knife into your back the minute it is turned.

One day we were talking about families. I told him how much I missed my wife and that I hoped she was missing me. I asked Gene about his family and he told me that he had just one son left now. He is a professional singer – 'not even country music'. He sings at weddings and concerts and is really quite successful at it.

'But we do not get along, he and I,' said Gene. 'As different as daylight and dark. But we are both too stubborn.'

I looked away for a while and let a few more acres of Oregon roll past. 'What happened to the others ?' I asked.

'I had a daughter, Cathy. Finest damn horse trainer I ever saw. When we were chasing cows she was always in the right place. I never needed to look and check, she was right there. But she has gone now.'

It must have been three minutes later when I asked what had happened to her. The details came out in short, bitter sentences. They came slowly, one at a time, without prompting from me but with time and miles between them, like a drip-feed of disaster and pain.

'She was murdered. Two years ago. Down in Texas. She had a Mexican boyfriend. I could tell as soon as I met him that he was no good. She wanted to leave him. He caught her packing her things. Didn't want her to go. Stabbed her.

'Cathy called me and I was going to come to get her but she said that she could handle the situation. Too brave, too stubborn. Like me.'

The conversation died, then a mile or more later he said, 'She did not recognise the murderous disposition of that person. I did. I should have taken care of her.'

'And where is the boyfriend now, the Mexican?'

'They caught him, cut-and-dried case of murder. He is out on bail of twelve hundred dollars. They do not want to convict him. They would have to give him life. He would be inside for fifty years. That would cost the state of Texas fifty thousand dollars a year – both of them from out of state you see.'

I asked Gene how it feels to know that the man responsible for his daughter's death is still a free man.

'I was going to take him there and then but an ex-service friend, Clayton Smith of the Texas Rangers, told me to wait and let the law take its course.'

It was odd to be talking of such bizarre things as we rode through the western landscape. By now the wagon train must have been three miles ahead. It had dropped out of sight into a dip in the road. The only trace of its presence was a ghost of a dust cloud. Our horses walked on side by side.

'And if he still does not end up in prison?'

'Then he is mine.'

I could not believe that I was actually having this conversation. The whole exchange was unreal. There was no doubt that Gene intended to follow through, to do what he said he would do. And it would not take any great detective work to find out that Gene was responsible for the Mexican's death. Then what? As Gene said, his experiences in Korea had made him determined that no one would ever take away his gun or lock a door on him. I hope, for the Mexican's sake, whoever he may be, that the law does take its course.

My reverie was broken by the sound of pounding hooves as the whole herd of horses and mules came thundering past my tent. I hoped that they would not get so excited that they would bash into the tent. Mules have a highly developed sense of self-preservation and I felt safe from them. I mentally ran through the list of horses and decided that of the lot only Roland would be stupid enough to try running over my tent. The animals soon settled down again. I fell asleep to the gentle sound of twenty contented equines tearing at the fresh grass. I was happy that we had finally made it out of the desert and into the green of Oregon.

It would be nice to be right just once in a while.

21

Ghostly pianist, boiling point and horizontal entertainment

We had not seen the last of the heat and the dry. The following night we stayed at Baker City rodeo ground, a desperately dry and dusty place. Every time a vehicle drove into the rodeo ground it was followed by an immense cloud of dust.

From Baker onwards we followed the Interstate 84 for almost a week but Ray had been applying himself to the job of trail boss and he had managed to find back roads to keep us off the actual motorway. The daytime temperatures stayed high, although the air was dry and it was cool at night. One of Ray's little detours took us past an incongruous building called the Hot Lake Hotel. It looks like a Brighton seafront hotel but sitting in the middle of a steaming swamp. The hotel is built on the site of a huge sulphur hot spring. It had been an Indian holy place where different tribes could meet to trade and talk peace on neutral territory – it is hard to feel war-like when you are stark naked and up to your neck in warm water. Perhaps the United Nations could learn a thing or two from the American Indians and flood the main council chamber.

The emigrants used to stop for a quick wash and brush up at Hot Lake. At the turn of the century its development as a health spa was started and all through the twenties and thirties a huge stream of the rich and the famous came there for rest, recuperation, good food and an exciting social life.

Then the social popularity of such places started to wane and Hot Lake Hotel became a rest home and hospital. Then it moved even further down market and became an old people's home. Now it is close to being nothing at all. A small wing is open where people can take long hot sulphurous baths. There is also a steam room. The rest of the impressive building is falling down; the loft and the upper floors have been given over to the pigeons and a ghost who plays the piano. The bulldozer is waiting for the current owner to run out of money, or hope, or both.

Our luck in staying off the freeway ran out at La Grande. There was only one way out to the west through the Blue Mountains and that was occupied by Interstate 84. We spent an unpleasant morning slogging up a steep motorway hill with lorries chucking out dirt and fumes as they strained and roared their discontent at the steepness of the hill. The railway takes the same route. It is so steep that they split the trains in half and put an extra couple of engines in the middle. The fact that modern methods of transport still take the same route as the Oregon Trail shows that the people who pioneered the trail really knew what they were doing.

The morning dragged on for ever because of the constant traffic and continuous uphill work. The road crash and death of the woman in Idaho had sharpened our sense of danger. Some of the drivers speeding down the hill on the opposite side of the freeway stared at us for fifteen seconds or more without looking at the road ahead.

After lunch we were able to get off the freeway and tootle along the old highway at our own sweet quiet pace. By then we were into the Blue Mountains, where there were trees, grass, foxgloves and bears. We even saw a mountain lion dashing across the road in front of the wagon train. That night was the first time that I had ever felt insecure in the tent. I hoped that the horses and mules which were ground-tethered all around the tent would alert me to any dangers. I kept a saucepan and stirrup iron close to my head so that I could make a big noise to scare off any predators with a taste for Englishmen. It was the only time during the whole trip that I wished I had taken the precaution of obtaining a gun.

The next day started cool and clear. There was a real dew on the grass. I even wore my coat. We came through the pass at Meacham and looked down to see a panorama of hot yellow wheat-land. We had entered a huge slice of Oregon which receives a mere ten inches of rain a year. The farmers get one measly crop of wheat every other year. The land is left brown, dusty and fallow for the other year. We could see huge tractors aimlessly stirring the dust in the sepia panorama in front of us. This was the third time we had been fooled into believing that we had seen the last of the desert conditions. I was beginning to pine for the lush landscape of Britain.

At the very top of the old freeway is a garage called Boiling Point. It was cool and breezy when we were there but as we came down off the bluff the temperature began to rise and rise until it was hovering close to 100° F.

We spent that night in Pendleton. At the turn of the century it was a real boom town – thanks to the gold coming in from the surrounding mountains. Again, it was the Chinese who supplied the labour. They were brought in to Oregon on five-year contracts. Recruiters went to mainland China promising undreamt of wealth; the Chinese were offered passage to America, a modest living allowance while they were there and then a lump sum and their passage home at the end. The young Chinese men came and found undreamt of oppression, exploitation and degradation. There are stories of whole Chinese mining crews being wiped out in terrible mining explosions which, strangely enough, tended to involve mining crews which were coming to the end of their contracts. Conveniently, these 'accidents' saved the mine-owners from paying the men off.

The Oregon ranchers and white miners thought it tremendous sport to deprive a Chinaman of his pigtail – a talisman as important to Chinese dignity as clothes are to a westerner. And in one infamous incident a ranch hand just pulled his gun and shot a Chinaman dead in the street. His defence was that he was drunk and felt like shooting the man. He was charged with discharging his firearm within the city limits, given a pathetically small fine and sent off home.

It is hardly surprising that the Chinese community of Pendleton retreated underground. The town once had a complete subterranean city: shops, restaurants, opium dens, laundries. The Chinese could move around town without ever coming to the surface. They even had their own judiciary system because the white courts would not recognise a crime committed by one Chinese against another.

Pendleton used to provide a comprehensive range of services to the mining community, extending to 'horizontal entertainment'. At one time the town boasted thirteen brothels. They flourished right through to the 1950s. Then it was brought to a sudden halt by a new preacher. One Monday morning, about three weeks after his arrival in Pendleton, he was on the telephone to the mayor. The preacher said that he had managed to compile two lists of names. One included all the active prostitutes in town, the other included all their active clients. He gave the mayor a week to get the prostitutes out of town. If the women were still in business, an advertisement would be appearing in the local paper. It would be an expensive advert but the preacher assured the mayor that there would be enough space on it for the names of the most important participants. Within seven days all the brothels had closed down. Some women left the area completely, others settled at Reith, four miles west of Pendleton. The local taxi-drivers did very well.

The 150 miles between Pendleton and a town called The

Dalles was through an endless sea of wheat-land. The temperatures were the highest of the trip. There was no shade for day after day. Looking across the horizon it was possible to see upwards of a dozen small whirlwinds working their way across the land. They ranged in diameter from a few feet to fifty or sixty feet across. Each one pulled a column of dust up into the already hazy air. By the end of the day, the dust had penetrated our clothes, our sinuses and the coats of our horses. At times we could see nothing other than the dust, the dusty wheatland and the dusty road ahead of us.

One night we were camped beside a river and were struck by a terrible windstorm. Some of the animals were tethered down by the river-bed where they could get some grass. I was glad that Rocky and Roland and a few others were up in a pasture on higher ground. I snuggled down in my sleeping bag and tried to cover my face against the choking dust which was getting in everywhere. Each lungful burnt my nose and throat as it went down. The tent began to rock more vigorously and I was worried that the pegs would pull free, so I went out in my underpants to knock in a few extra ones. I looked over to see Jesse and Ralph moving their animals to safety on high ground. It looked like a scene from hell as the men struggled with their frightened animals in the poor visibility. The wind-blown sand stung my bare back and legs. I was just knocking in the last extra peg when I felt a prickling sensation around my legs and halfway up my back. I thought I was being attacked and enveloped by a swarm of insects. In fact I had been goosed by a lump of itinerant tumble weed.

It was just one week from the end of the trip, at a town called Wasco, that we had our first, and last, fist fight. There had been tensions between people on the wagon train before but they had been quite minor. Ray was under extra stress because an old injury in his left leg was starting to play up. Initially he had kept riding through the pain but it had become so bad for a few days that he had to stop riding and went over to driving a support vehicle. Until then, he had ridden every step of the way from the Missouri river. For him it was a dream ruined. Jesse was getting tired. Gene had kept clear of it all, Harold had been doing his best to stay friends with everyone. Even Ralph was getting a bit tetchy. We were all coming to realise that we were going to finish soon. We had to prepare ourselves for life after this was all over – but the euphoria of actually finishing was not yet upon us. We were all beginning to wonder whether it had all been worthwhile.

The day of the fight, Ray had just finished fixing yet another puncture on the truck – the third that week. He and Jesse were discussing the next day's route. Jesse did not seem to be that interested and said, 'Whatever flicks your wick old man.' Within seconds the two of them were trying to knock hell out of each other. There were enough other men around to stop the fight before more than three or four blows had been landed but the sight of two grandfathers, men you have come to know and love over the past two months, trying to injure each other is not a pleasant one. It still makes me sad to think of the incident even now.

The next day was a short one. Just eighteen miles down to the gorge of the Columbia river. We had hoped to be able to stay at an Oregon state camp site but the superintendent there did not want us – regulations and all that you know. Proof positive that we were getting close to civilisation and its attendant respect for bureaucracy and bureaucrats.

We pressed on and managed to find ourselves a wonderful camp site with a great view. It was well up on the hills overlooking the Columbia Gorge. The Columbia river used to be a magnificent thundering mass of white water with the occasional placid section between rapids. It had carved its deep gorge over the passing millennia using the power of the water collected from an area easily six times the size of Britain. For the pioneers who had spent so many weeks crossing the endlessly scrubby and water-hungry lands of Idaho and eastern Oregon, the sight of it must have been both wonderful and terrifying. The last hundred miles of their trip was on rafts down this dangerous torrent of water and many lives were lost.

The pioneers would hardly recognise the river as it is today. The Columbia is now a major producer of hydro-electricity. It has been dammed and dammed again until it has been stripped, emasculated, robbed of its former power and glory. The once mighty river is now a series of placid lakes reflecting the blue of the cloudless sky. Where white-water canoeists would have feared to go, huge grain barges now chug their way up and down what remains of the stream. A feeling of the past power of the river can only be found down by the outlets from the dams. Here the water of the Columbia bursts briefly and angrily back into the world, white and roaring for a few seconds before being mixed with, and pacified by, the still waters of the next reservoir. And even this brief outburst of power is not what it used to be. The flow of the Columbia has been yet further reduced by the sucking and guzzling of a million aluminium pipes which feed the clicking, spurting and dribbling of a billion irrigation nozzles. The water which has fallen in wasteful torrents on the western foothills of the Rockies has been carefully metered out to the wheat, vegetable and grass-land farmers of the Pacific North-west – a greater calling, more useful to mankind, but at the cost of destroying one of nature's most magnificent setpiece spectacles. The dramatic gorge is certainly less impressive now that it has just a long lake in its bottom rather than a massive river.

A major beneficiary of the damming has been the wind-surfing fraternity. A few miles downstream of us, where the Hood river joins the Columbia, is possibly the world's best, most reliable windsurfing centre. The cool air off the Pacific

Ocean comes inland and finds the desert on the other side of the Cascade Mountains. There it rises, sucking in yet more cool air behind it. The Columbia Gorge funnels the wind along the lake, producing good consistent twenty-, thirty- or forty-mile-an-hour winds blowing over flat water – perfect conditions for the rubber-suited hedonists to bash from one side of the river to the other.

We pulled into our camp site at about five-thirty in the evening. It was the usual desert pasture of sage brush and dust but this one was three hundred feet above the river and offered views of the sweeps of the gorge both east and west. A dirt track ran through our pasture and up along the edge of a steep-sided valley. We pulled the wagons off the track and on to a small level area set like a footstep in the side of the valley. A second dirt track ran off to the left and down towards a small summer stream which trickled through the valley bottom about a quarter of a mile from the camp site.

I had been riding Roland that day so I was leading Rocky. I took both horses down for a drink and to wash the dust out of their throats. It was a nice spot and the water looked clear enough for me to drink but I had been warned again and again not to trust American streams. Rocky and Roland slurped noisily while I squatted down and dabbled my fingers in the cool water. It felt wonderful. I cupped my hands and splashed some over the back of my sun-scorched neck – as seen in scores of cowboy films. I filled my hat with water and put it back on my head. It is not the sort of thing you do when anyone is watching. It must have been chance but Roland looked at me and sighed. I climbed on to his back and walked the horses up towards the camp site.

As we came around the corner I saw that one of the wagons was heading away from the camp straight up the hill. I wondered for a moment why it was going so fast. It then swung abruptly to the right to circle around the top of the camp site. As it came I saw that Ralph's wagon seat was empty. It was a runaway. Both of Ralph's mustangs and his young mule Buster were on his triple hitch and all three were running as fast as they could go. I became aware of the pandemonium in the camp ground. Ralph was legging it across to try to intercept the wagon and grab one of the trailing lines. The two mustangs had a wild, white-rimmed look of terror in their eyes and Buster, hitched to one side, was more or less being dragged along by their panic. Ralph launched himself into the air in a desperate attempt to grab one of the flailing lines. It was a splendid effort and would have earned him a creditable reputation as a brave and agile goalie had he been born in the right country. But he missed, fell over and was lucky not to get hit by a flailing hoof or even by the wagon itself. The team swung around and started heading straight for the side of Jesse's rig.

When blind panic takes control of the brain of a horse its legs will start to run, it does not matter where, just as long as it is running somewhere. Perhaps in the primeval plains just running anywhere is good enough. A dash into a dangerous place might even be a survival tactic. The carnivorous pursuer would be merely after its next meal while the horse would be running for the sake of all future meals. The lion or wolf might just decide that it was not worthwhile carrying on the chase down through a deep ravine or through deep water. Sante Fe and Yuma were concentrating hard on getting their legs to propel them as fast as possible. Their heads contained nothing other than blind screaming panic. Horses are extremely good at panic.

The difference between horses and mules extends well beyond the length of the ears – there are also differences in what goes on between the ears. Even while mules are running away they have enough brain power left to do a modicum of thinking. For people this is not always a good thing. A ridden horse and ridden mule might both flee in fear from a bear or a cougar. But while the horse brain has nothing but fear in it, the mule might, just possibly, have a plan. While the horse is merely running and taking his rider with him, the mule might be prepared to take a minor diversion towards a tree on which to wipe off his rider, thereby increasing his own chances of survival. Mules have a much better developed sense of self-preservation than horses. A horse can be bullied, whipped and spurred into a dangerous situation – a mule will dig his or her heels in and not move.

Buster's body was doing overtime in trying to keep up with Yuma and Sante Fe. His brain was working extremely hard as well. He was the only one of the three giving any thought to the subject of navigation. He was doing his best to save himself. He could see that they were heading straight for the side of Jesse's wagon and he was shoving his shoulder good and hard into Yuma in an effort to steer his panicky team-mates away from danger and inevitable injury. His bright little eyes popped with the effort as he shoved even harder at Yuma's heaving flank. His little legs were hard pressed just trying to keep up with the bigger mustangs, let alone the extra effort of trying to steer them out of danger. For a moment it looked as though his shoving would force the horses clear and not leave a big enough gap for him to squeeze through but at the last moment his body made a cunning little snaking motion and he scraped past the back corner of Jesse's wagon. The team was then clear and heading for the open sage-brush. But this was not good enough for Buster, as the stout shrubs of sage still represented a risk of injury. He stopped pushing at his team-mates and started dragging them the other way, over towards the dirt track which led up and away along the valley edge over the crest of a hill.

I sat immobile on Roland as I watched them go. Then I realised that I was the only one still on horseback and in a position to give chase. I let go of Rocky's lead rope and urged Roland off up the hill in pursuit of the wagon. I did not have much of a plan of action. I remember briefly wishing that I had been riding the more sure-footed Rocky. He would be more reliable in a tight squeeze; he could also run a lot faster.

John Wayne's stunt man would gallop up alongside a runaway stage-coach and jump on to the lead team. I did not think for one moment that I could do the same thing – not without practice anyway – but I did think I might be able to get alongside and grab a line or two while I shouted something suitable. 'Whoa' might have been appropriate for the situation. But getting alongside would be next to impossible given the narrowness of the track.

That left the back door approach, which would entail jumping in through the back of the heaving, lurching wagon, moving forward and in a synchronised action applying the brakes and pulling on the reins. This was not actually a manoeuvre I particularly fancied attempting. Besides, Roland is a big coward and I knew that as soon as we got close enough to the wagon he would start to veer away from it. At that moment I began to be glad that I was riding Roland and stood almost no chance of getting anywhere near the damn thing.

We galloped up the track through the cloud of dust thrown up by the pounding hooves and spinning wheels. I noticed all sorts of debris which had been thrown out of Ralph's wagon as it bounced off the rocks and sage-brush stems. I saw my camera lying at the side of the track – the telephoto lens was hanging off at a sickening angle even before it disappeared under Roland's steel-tipped hooves. As we thundered over it I thought, 'Why does it have to be my bloody camera?'

I still had no clear idea of what I would do should I catch the wagon – though I knew, with some relief, that I stood no chance of that anyway. On Rocky I could probably have got close – close enough for me to injure myself in a foolish and almost certainly futile attempt at stopping the runaway team.

The wagon bashed on along the track with me following thirty yards behind. I could not see the mustangs but I could still see Buster on his side hitch, ears flat against his head, alternately pushing and pulling at Yuma as he struggled to keep the wagon running straight. Eventually, the outer wheels of the wagon slipped over towards the valley side of the path and the wagon-bed finally parted company from the chassis. The whole lot was brought rapidly to a halt in a big patch of sage. I arrived a couple of seconds later, jumped off Roland and grabbed hold of the team to wait until help arrived. Actually all three animals were too winded to go anywhere. I think the sequence of events would have been exactly the same had I been there or not.

It was not long before a puffing crowd of wagon trainers came up the hill. We were terribly lucky; neither Yuma nor Sante Fe nor Buster was seriously injured – a few cuts and scrapes was all. Even the wagon was not badly damaged – the bolts connecting the bed to the chassis had sheered off nice and clean leaving both sections more or less undamaged. The hydraulic brake lines had been well mangled and a few harness straps had been broken but it was nothing that could not be sorted out in a few hours.

It turned out that Ralph had driven his team to a place which he thought would be a good level spot to stop. He got down and started to unhitch them when he decided that just moving them forwards a couple more feet would give him a level bed for the night. He decided to be lazy. Instead of climbing back into the driver's seat he coaxed them forwards from the ground. Something rattled or bumped in the wagon and they were away. He had managed to hold on to Sante Fe's halter for a while but he had to let go before being dragged under a wheel. I had come around the corner just before his second attempt to grab the traces.

We were lucky that no one was injured, as a runaway team will certainly not stop to avoid a pedestrian. Three hours of hard work saw the wagon back in one piece and ready for the road again.

It was an uphill struggle getting any sympathy for my wrecked camera. It was the best one I had ever owned, bought just for the trip. The insurance claim should make interesting reading.

22

Slugs at last, a Scottish piper and a horse called Dylan

We took our last rest day at The Dalles on the Columbia river. It was in the forests around The Dalles that the emigrants cut the timber for the massive rafts needed to carry their wagons the hundred miles down river to Oregon City. The cattle and stock would be driven along a narrow track which ran beside the river. The pioneer diaries tell-heartrending stories of fatal accidents on this final stage of the trip. To have come two thousand miles, to have witnessed the deaths and sacrifice of so many people and animals, only to die in this last tiny section of the journey was the tragic fate of many of the pioneers.

An entrepreneur called Barlowe decided that he would make some money by building a road through the Cascade Mountains which lay between The Dalles and the coast. The people who live in the The Dalles claim that their town is the real end of the Oregon Trail. People who question this claim are asked how people got from The Dalles to Oregon City.

'Along the river or the Barlowe Trail,' is the obvious and inevitable reply. This answer will be greeted with a smirk of intellectual triumph as a point is proven. The Dalles may well mark the end of the trail but it was never the end of the journey. The Dalles is not the promised land – that lies on the other side of the Cascade Mountains.

After our rest day we took the wagons up the steep hill

behind The Dalles and into the mountains. As we climbed, we came across more grass and more trees. We were assured by the locals that we had left the heat and the dust behind for good. We had been disappointed so often that we were scared to believe them. The people of eastern Oregon make jokes about those who are foolish enough to live in the wet area on the other side of the Cascade Mountains.

'First the bad news: forty people fell off their bicycles in Portland yesterday. Now the good news: only seventeen of them were drowned.'

We spent that night in a woodland camp site. There was a sad end of term feeling coming over us. Two more nights on the road and we would be riding into Oregon City. We would each have to deal with the question as to whether or not it had all been worth it.

We started that morning in bright sunshine. Within three hours we were in dripping, dank, dark-green forest. Impossibly tall trees cut out what little light there had been. Ferns grew tall and lush along the side of the road. A stream came tumbling down the mountainside at every bend in the road. I noticed a big black juicy slug at the side of the road. It was wonderful. I vowed never to complain about our British climate again. No wonder the English felt so much at home in Oregon and had wanted to hold on to it.

Someone, somewhere, made a mistake and we travelled thirty-seven miles that day. We finished it tired but elated.

Two more days to go; and as we came down out of the Cascade Mountains the trees gave way to real English-looking hedgerows. None of the roads went in straight lines, the pastures were full of luscious deep grass, the cattle looked fat and slick, not the scrawny range cows we had seen since leaving Nebraska. The blackberries were so thick on the bushes that they hung like bunches of grapes. They tasted sweet and succulent. By this stage in their journey the emigrants must have been thinking that it had all been worthwhile. But they must also have been daunted by the amount of timber they would have to clear away before they could plant their crops.

My mind kept on swinging from joy to mild depression. Soon it would all be over. I would leave these people on the wagon train. Paula who had left her husband back in Illinois – faith like a rock and a voice like an angel. Harold whose pumping heart was letting him down but whose spirit was strong enough to keep him going. Ray who had dreamed of this trip through half a century on the road. Jesse who had said he would do it and who did it because he was a man of his word. He would go back east and finish the last section of his continental expedition. Caroline who was here because of her love of her husband Jesse, because she subscribed to the old idea that her husband's ambition was her own. Then Betty who really did not seem to know why she was here except to try to make a bit of money.

I wondered if we had been cruel to our animals to expect them to undertake such a feat. It was the mules and the horses who had done the real work. But we had all done our best to look after them. They looked pretty good. They were lean but not too thin. Work-hardened.

I began to savour every moment in the saddle. Rocky with his athletic willingness to please and his mad look, that readiness to tackle anything and everything. Roland with his steady, steady continent-crossing walk. I was beginning to appreciate his measured paces. Given time, he could have made the whole trip, his beautiful head nodding through the miles. I would miss them and felt a debt to them. I needed to find them good homes. They had both finished the trip in better condition than I could have hoped. I asked everyone I met if they wanted to buy a good horse.

We spent the last night at a farm just seven miles outside Oregon City. One of the neighbours came over to see the wagon train and Harold mentioned to her that I had two horses for sale. Donna had three kids and was looking for a horse which both she and her kids could ride. She looked

Rocky over and decided to buy him. It was a nice place, a good pasture with plenty of shelter and trees, good long grass and plenty of dew to keep his feet moist and supple. She planned to try Rocky out in cattle-cutting competitions. He would love it. She agreed to let me take him on the last bit of the trip.

The next day we rode the last seven miles and arrived at the marker-stone at the end of the trail at twelve noon on Friday, 30 August, exactly as Betty had planned it back on her kitchen table in Metropolis, Illinois – the town where eighty per cent of all the fly-swatters in America are made.

We were greeted by a modest crowd, a man playing the bagpipes and a few local dignitaries. After a few speeches and a group photograph – with the big cheeses who seldom miss an opportunity to appear in the local paper – it was all over. We spent the night camped out in the park with the horses and mules tethered to the trees. The local Chamber of Commerce laid on a barbecue for us.

We spent the Saturday preparing to go our separate ways. Jesse and Ralph were determined to take their wagons the remaining hundred miles to the sea, everyone else was heading back east to Missouri and Illinois. Donna came and took Rocky away. It was horrible seeing him go.

The next morning at eight o'clock Jesse and Ralph drove their wagons out of the park and headed off towards the coast – they were going to drive another hundred miles because they wanted 'to go for a paddle in the Pacific'. Harold, Ray, Betty and Paula loaded up their animals and headed off east in a small convoy. Our wagon train, like the hundreds before it, had broken apart. People were heading off in different directions. Many of the goodbyes were for ever. People who had forged links of friendship and interdependence were going their own ways.

I was left alone in the park with Roland hollering his loneliness. He was not the only one who was upset. I have never felt so alone in my life. I sat down on the grass to think of a way to get him a good home. I had decided to go and call one of the local TV stations to try to get some publicity for him when a car drove into the park. It was the lady who owned the farm where we had spent our last night on the road. She had seen Roland and liked the look of him and she had a fistful of dollars. He now lives in the field right next to Rocky. He is used as a saddle horse and he also pulls a one-horse buggy in parades. I bet he looks marvellous.

Sharon and Bill have renamed him. They call him Dylan. Poor confused horse.

About the Author

Dylan Winter has worked on and around farms since his late teens. He studied agricultural engineering at university. His journalistic career kicked off on *Farmers Weekly* and moved seamlessly to the BBC where he presented Farming Today – rising at 4.30 every morning.

He is now a general jobbing freelance with a passion for all things rural. He has always been involved with horses and this Oregon Trail ride is just on of many long distance rides which he has undertaken.

He believes that the human brain – well his anyway – is hard wired to travel at three miles an hour. At that speed he can absorb enough of the passing world to understand and appreciate it. Any faster and everything happens too quickly.

Dylan lives in a Buckinghamshire village with his wife and two children. He can often be seen riding his American Quarterhorse Mac – at three miles an hour – along the lanes and bridle ways of North Bucks. Following somewhere in their wake will be his laconic labrador.

Dylan is the author of two books and has presented radio and TV programmes on everything from Britain's canal system to corrupt dentists. His DVD programmes on logging and the American grain harvest have won admirers all over the world.

Other Titles from Old Pond Publishing

Two Thousand Mile Harvest   DYLAN WINTER

Dylan Winter follows ten of the world's largest combines on their five-month harvesting journey from Munday, Texas to Lethbridge, Alberta, in one of the most popular farm machinery films ever made. The Payne family and a crew of eighteen show just what life is like on the road. DVD

Custom Cutters   DYLAN WINTER

Dylan Winter returned to the American grain belt to film two more crews working their way north. The Fredericks run John Deere 9660STS combines and Kenworth trucks; the Farris brothers operate Case IH 2388 combines and immaculate Peterbilts. The programme includes informative interviews with the drivers, contractors and farmers. DVD

Loggers: from chainsaw to sawmill in British Columbia   DYLAN WINTER

Vancouver Island, British Columbia is the site of Dylan Winter's exciting programme that covers chainsaw work, yarding, extraction by truck, train and helicopter, dry-land sort, water transport and the Somas mill. DVD

Rocky Mountain Cowboys   DYLAN WINTER

Dylan Winter experiences part of the working year on the 250,000 acre Pitchfork Ranch, Wyoming, filming the cowboys as they summer pasture their cattle 8,000 feet up in the Rocky Mountains. He shows the full range of cattle ranching activities, including roping, bronc-busting, droving and working with horses, cattle, mules and the famous Blue Heeler cattle dogs. DVD

Juggernaut Drivers   LESLIE PURDON

1970s trucker Rich revels in the laughs and camaraderie of his life on the road. He sets up a transport company, North Kent, with two pals. They run legal when they can and cut corners when necessary, gamble on new trucks and are cheated out of their earnings – but still come up smiling. A lively and funny account of a fictional transport company. Paperback

Free complete catalogue:

Old Pond Publishing
Dencora Business Centre
36 White House Road, Ipswich IP1 5LT, United Kingdom
Phone: 01473 238200   Fax: 01473 238201
Website: www.oldpond.com
Email: enquiries@oldpond.com